COPING
WITH
CRITICISM

by

JAMIE
BUCKINGHAM

**LOGOS INTERNATIONAL
PLAINFIELD, NEW JERSEY**

COPING WITH CRITICISM
Copyright © 1978 by Logos International
All rights reserved
Printed in the United States of America
Library of Congress Catalog Card Number: 78-60994
International Standard Book Number: 0-88270-327-7
Logos International
Plainfield, New Jersey 07060

To:
My discerning wife
My painfully honest children
My exasperated secretary
The elders of the Tabernacle Church, Melbourne, Florida
The wonderful people (and a few grouches) who make up that body
And all others who have felt the call of God to criticize me. . .
Without your magnificent contribution this book would have been completed at least five years sooner.

Jamie Buckingham presents practical guides to successful living

CRITIC: One who detects and points out faults or defects.

CRITICIZE: In its basic sense suggests a discernment and judicial evaluation of both merits and faults. In ordinary use, however, commonly implies an unfavorable judgment or a pointing out of faults whether real or imagined. Often takes on the form of a severe rebuke.

COPE: To deal with on fairly even terms and manage to overcome problems and difficulties.

After years of reading—and writing—books, I have reached the conclusion that no one reads forewords or prefaces.

Therefore, to save us both a lot of trouble—and to keep down the criticism—I am not going to say anything.

—Jamie Buckingham
Melbourne, Florida

Contents

BOOK ONE

Truth and Consequences

As usual, we were running late. Way late. For months we had been promising our friends, Len and Catherine, we would arrive at their home no later than 2:00 P.M. It's a three-hour drive from our place in Melbourne down the east coast of Florida to their home in Boynton Beach. We intended to spend the afternoon visiting, then I was to speak at their Monday night prayer meeting. To arrive on time, we had to leave the house no later than 11:00 A.M.

But everything went wrong that morning. The phone rang incessantly. Someone had to take the dog to the vet. My secretary called and reminded me I had promised to get a short article in the mail no later than noon. And to top it all off, my wife, Jackie, decided we should stop by and pick up her mother to go with us.

We were already an hour late when we finally got our bags packed and jumped in the car. Only then did we discover it was nearly out of gas—which meant another ten minutes' delay. Then we had to pick up Jackie's mother—another fifteen minutes. By the time we were on the interstate we were an hour and a half late.

"We better stop and call ahead and let Len and Catherine know we're running late," Jackie said. "It will be at least three-thirty before we get there."

"There's a phone booth at the next exit," I said. "I'll wait in the car while you make the call."

Jackie looked at me. "Why don't I wait in the car while you call. That should be a man's job. Anyway, it's raining."

"If I called I'd probably blame you for making us late," I said, ignoring her objections.

"Why blame anyone?" my simplistic wife asked, looking at me innocently through her big glasses. "Why not just say we were late getting away?"

I have a terrible time with questions like that. We drove silently for almost a mile, listening to the slap-slap of the worn-out windshield blades. "If I don't blame someone then I'll be criticized," I finally confessed. "I can't stand being criticized."

"You know Len isn't going to criticize you," Jackie said.

"Well, he'll *think* criticism, even if he doesn't say it," I said.

We pulled up at the phone booth and with an "I wish you'd grow up one of these days," Jackie got out of the car in the rain and called Len to break the news.

No problem. It turned out our friends were running late themselves. Even so, I couldn't help but wonder how I would ever make it in life unless I had someone to blame things on—my wife, mother, or associates.

Maybe it's my insecurity. Maybe it's my fear of rejection. Whatever it is, in times past I have been devastated by criticism. Just the slightest correction would give me blinding headaches. And harsh criticism, the kind that comes when some angry woman calls on the phone and strikes at me from her own personal hurt—accusing me of insensitivity, thoughtlessness, and cruelty—would send me into a depression which could last for days.

Across the years I learned it was easier to run from criticism than cope with it. I would go to any length to escape having to hear it. If I knew the caller on the phone was going to criticize me, I would ask Jackie to take the call. Then I would go in the bathroom, turn on the water, and rattle papers so I wouldn't have to hear what was being said. It was all a matter of evasion—putting up a huge smoke screen to blot out something unpleasant.

I have hidden in the back room of the house when I saw certain persons coming up the front walk. I have forced the children to answer the phone rather than face some irate critic on the other end of the line. I have refused to read letters from people I knew were writing to disagree with me. In fact, there were times when I even refused to open them, thinking if their criticisms remained in the envelope they wouldn't jump out and hurt me.

I have acted tough, played humble, and blamed others. I have used phrases like, "Gee, I didn't know anything about that." Or, "I tried to get the elders of the church to change that, but—" Or, "Remember, several editors tampered with it before it got into print."

For years I have refused to read published reviews of my books. Very early in my writing career I discovered I couldn't handle them. If the reviews were good, then I would swell up like a frog sitting on a rock in the middle of a pond. Despite my "Aw, shucks," response, inwardly I croaked with pride. There were times when I actually clipped a rave review and left it lying around the house so some visitor would see how important his host actually was.

On the other hand, if the reviews were bad—calling my style "juvenile," pointing out my lack of spiritual understanding, criticizing my limited vocabulary, or calling my writing, as one reviewer did, "at best, mediocre"—I would go to pieces. Either I would lie awake late into the night, thinking how I could answer the reviewer with sarcasm (I never did, however) or I would slip quietly into a deep depression vowing I would never again write another book or article.

Regardless of the flavor of the review, though, I was rendered ineffective. So, like the letters, phone calls, and angry people ringing my front door bell, I found it safer just to ignore them.

Running from unpleasantries in order to escape criticism is a problem nearly all of us have faced at one time or another.

At the weekly meeting of the Council of Elders in our church, one of the men asked the rest of us to pray for him. "I've been through a time of deep self-examination," he explained. "It started with a dream. In the dream I was standing in my house looking out at a huge oak tree in the front lawn. Its spreading branches gave shade to the entire house. As I looked, a man appeared with a big drill and bored a precise hole, about two inches in diameter, through the heart of the tree. From my position in the house I could see all the way through the oak tree. Shortly after that, the whole top of the tree toppled over, and the shade was gone."

As he spoke I looked around the room at the other men, examining their faces. All of them probably had some kind of interpretation for the dream, I thought. But the man speaking was a recognized expert in the area of dreams and their interpretation. The other men, like myself, remained silent—eager, no doubt, to see if their interpretation was the same as the expert's.

He went ahead to say that as he meditated on the dream, he realized the oak tree referred to character. And in his case, there was a hole through his character which represented some kind of flaw, or character deficiency.

"I knew what that hole was," he continued. "From childhood I have fought a battle to overcome a fierce tendency in my life—a tendency to tell people what they want to hear rather than tell them the truth."

His problem, of course, was obvious. To tell the truth means exposing yourself to evaluation by others. "Who do you think you are to correct me. Look at your own life!" In fact, once a man begins to tell the truth, he is often accused of judging, which opens the door for people to throw Scripture verses back at him in machine gun style. "Judge not that ye be not judged." "First cast out the beam out of thine own eye; and then shalt thou see clearly to cast out the mote out of thy brother's eye."

Not only that, but telling the truth means running the risk of having to defend the truth—and of being criticized because of it. Therefore, sooner or later most of us find it easier to tell people what they want to hear, than to speak the truth.

"When I saw that," he continued, "and when I brought the Lord into the setting, I realized he wanted to set me free from this damning tendency which has caused me to be a chronic liar when it came to speaking truth to others."

He then told us that as he meditated on this subject, he asked himself the question, "When did this tendency begin?"

That stimulated his memory. He recalled a little scene when he was four years old. His family was living in Oregon at the time, and he was the youngest of nine children. He had a little playmate, a girl, who was about the same age. One day his mother discovered the two of them playing in the bathroom. It was an innocent experience, but somehow in their play activity they had gone into the bathroom and closed the door. As a result of this episode he was not only punished by his mother—who was a very loving woman—but was ridiculed and teased by his older brothers. From that time on, he said, he determined that in order to escape punishment and ridicule he would try to please people. This was easy to do since he had a wonderful mother whom he loved to please—even at the cost of telling the truth.

Listening to my friend talk about his problem—which was my problem too, even though my mother never caught me locked in the bathroom with a little girl—made me realize that the fear of criticism is a tremendously motivating force in the lives of most people. Afraid to face people because of how they might react, I either told lies or I reacted in anger—which was simply another defense mechanism.

I thought back to a time several weeks before. It was at another elders' meeting. We were discussing a new project I felt the church should assume. Several times during the meeting I glanced over at my friend. His brow was wrinkled and he twisted his hands nervously as he asked a few questions. I sensed he was reluctant to give his approval. Had I been more discerning I would have realized he felt we were heading in the wrong direction, yet his desire to please those around him, especially those in authority, was even larger than his desire to speak truth and save us from difficult consequences. Thus he simply sat back, wrinkled his brow, and said very little.

However, the next day he left a note in my mailbox. It was a blistering kind of warning. He pointed out several legitimate objections to my project—things I sincerely wished he had brought up in the meeting the day before. He then concluded by saying we were moving too fast and needed to slow down.

I was shocked, not so much by his conclusions (which I recognized as valid) but by his boldness. It seemed to be out of character for my soft-spoken friend.

However, my own reluctance to engage in a face-to-face confrontation kept me from doing what I should have done—which was to call him on the phone and say, "Hey, what's this all about?"

As I considered his weakness—the hole in the tree, so to speak—I realized my own hole was even bigger. As far back as I could remember, I had a difficult time saying no. Like my friend, I said yes when I should have said no because I wished to please.

Especially was this true when it came to personal confrontations which might put me on the defensive. The problem often surfaced in strange places, such as filling out my calendar schedule for the coming year.

I had told my secretary, Laura Watson, that I was going to take only three days a month for outside speaking engagements. The rest of the time I planned to stay home, writing and fulfilling my duties to the congregation in Melbourne.

Laura greeted my announcement with a skeptical smile.

She knew me.

Sure enough, before long my calendar had filled up—far

beyond my planned three days a month. My problem was most apparent when my friends approached me, asking me to come speak, conduct a seminar, or teach at a conference. Perfect strangers I could handle. But when it came to a long time friend who put pressure on me, I would invariably give in and tell him yes. Before long I had an out-of-town trip planned during almost every week for the coming year. There was hardly time left to come home and speak to my children, much less sit down and write a book.

"Why don't you let me handle your engagements?" Laura asked in desperation. "Why is it so hard for you to say no to all these people?"

"I hate to hurt their feelings," I said.

"I think there's more to it than that," she said with a knowing look.

I thought of the words of Isaiah, words which I had longed to appropriate in my life, but had been unable to do so because I feared criticism.

> The Lord God has given me his words of wisdom so that I may know what I should say to all these weary ones. Morning by morning he wakens me and opens my understanding to his will. The Lord God has spoken to me and I have listened; I do not rebel nor turn away. I give my back to the whip, and my cheeks to those who pull out the beard. I do not hide from shame—they spit in my face.
>
> Because the Lord God helps me, I will not be dismayed: therefore, I have set my face like flint to do his will, and I know that I will triumph. He who gives me justice is near. Who will dare to

fight against me now? Where are my enemies? Let them appear! See, the Lord God is for me! Who shall declare me guilty? All my enemies shall be destroyed like old clothes eaten up by moths! (Isaiah 50:4-9 The Living Bible)

I realized I would never have this confidence as long as I ran from confrontation. Some place along the path I would have to stop and set my face like flint to do His will—and speak His truth, no matter the consequences.

In the meantime, I told Laura to go ahead and tell everyone who called, wanting me to write their book or come speak to their assembly, that I had taken all the work I could for the foreseeable future.

But it wasn't the busyness that was causing me to set my secretary out in front like a shield to catch all the spears and darts—it was my own cowardliness. I was afraid to say no. I knew the minute I allowed myself to get into a face-to-face confrontation I would buckle. I knew the moment I started speaking truth I would have to bear the consequences.

It finally happened. An old acquaintance, a man from Michigan who had on several occasions in the past tried to get me to come speak at his church, finally got through to me. I was sitting at Laura's desk when the phone rang. She was busy at the file cabinet so I answered the phone.

"This must be of the Lord," my old acquaintance boomed. "Every time I've called before I've gotten your secretary. She refuses to let me get through to you. I kept telling my wife I knew you weren't that busy—at least not so busy you didn't have time for your old friends."

I felt the fear knotting my stomach. "I've been out of town a lot," I stammered.

"See, I knew that was the case. Some guys are afraid to answer their phone. They've outgrown us little fellows. They surround themselves with all kinds of functionaries who do their dirty work for them. But I knew you weren't like that. You're too real. Too honest. You'd never push your old friends aside just because you've become famous."

I gave a little nervous laugh on the phone. Laura had finished at the filing cabinet and was standing across the desk, looking at me. Her lips were pursed, causing a little white ring around the mouth. "L-e-t m-e t-a-l-k t-o h-i-m," she mouthed. But it was too late.

"You've been putting me off for years," my old friend rattled on. "I'll not take no for an answer. You've been saying yes to everyone else. Now just name the date. Anytime between now and the end of the year."

"I can't come on a Sunday," I said nervously.

I heard Laura sigh. She was shaking her head vigorously. But I couldn't back down, not now. He'd criticize me.

"You don't have to come on a Sunday. Just give us three days during the week."

Laura was busy scribbling something on a pad. She held it up for me to read. "TELL HIM YOU'LL CHECK YOUR CALENDAR AND WRITE HIM BACK."

I felt a great weight lift from my shoulders.

"I don't have my calendar with me," I stammered truthfully. "I'll check and see if I have a clear date and write you back."

"Okay!" he said laughing. "Now remember, I won't take no for an answer. I'll expect a letter from you within the week."

I hung up the phone and sat staring at the receiver like

it was a rattlesnake which had tried to bite me and I had finally managed to stun it with a stick. Suddenly it rang again. I leaped out of the chair and motioned for Laura to pick it up. I wasn't about to get struck again.

She handled it like the pro she is.

"I'm sorry. Mr. Buckingham would love to come, especially since you're an old friend. But he has promised the Lord to stay home and work on several book projects and to spend some time with his family and the local church. He's taken all the engagements he can handle for the foreseeable future. Why don't you write him a letter and tell him you love him? That would mean a lot since he's under a great deal of pressure right now."

"Why can't I do that?" I moaned, when she hung up the phone after a pleasant goodbye conversation.

"Because you're a coward," Laura said, matter-of-factly.

"What do you mean?"

"I mean you know what is right. You know what God has told you to do. But you're afraid to tell people."

"You're right," I groaned.

"What are you going to write the man in Michigan?"

"I'll have no trouble with that," I said confidently. "I'll simply write him and tell him I have established certain priorities and cannot come to Michigan this year."

"Do you feel you are supposed to go to Michigan next year?"

"No."

"Are you going to say that in the letter?"

"Well, er, ah, probably not. It's better to say my calendar is full and he should contact me next year."

"Then you'll have to go through this whole thing again next year. Why don't you just tell him the truth? Tell him you are trying to be obedient to God and do not feel he is leading you to come to Michigan."

"But that makes it sound like I don't like him," I said.

Laura took a keen look at me. "Do you like him?"

"Sure. He's not only an old friend, but I feel he's a devoted man of God."

"If you really like him, tell him the truth. If you're going to lie to anyone, lie to your enemies. Not your friends."

I thought of what my fellow elder had said about wanting to please people more than he wanted to tell the truth. My tree had a hole in it too. In fact, it had already fallen down on top of my house. From some place out of the past I remember my father quoting Sir Walter Scott:

> "Oh, what a tangled web we weave,
> When first we practice to deceive!"

I wondered, though, if Sir Walter had to contend with criticism the way I do.

In short, for a number of years, I did everything I could to escape criticism.

I don't do that any more. At least, I don't do it as much as I used to. Instead, I have worked out a system which is helping me solve my problem. Not only that, but the system has helped me overcome a number of character flaws which I figured I'd just have to carry with me to my grave. It's not that I now enjoy being criticized. A person has to have a sick mind to enjoy that kind of thing—especially if the criticism is justified. But I am learning after all these years how to cope with criticism.

And that's what this book is all about.

2

Bite Your Tongue

It took a long time before I recognized there is a difference between coping with criticism and being immune to it. A couple of years ago, after having gone through several moderate encounters with angry people—and not going into depression or getting angry in return—I began to feel I had at last conquered my old problem.

One Friday, speaking at a ladies' luncheon, I began my remarks by announcing that they were looking at a man who had finally become immune to criticism.

It was an audacious thing to say!

It was also an extremely foolish thing to say.

Mortals have a difficult time understanding what is going on in the spiritual world (what the Bible calls "the heavenlies"). If we did understand, we'd be mighty careful about playing the braggadocio. The purpose of God's visitation on earth, the purpose of the Bible being written, the purpose of the Holy Spirit in the world today is that we might be conformed to the image of God's Son. At least, if I understand Romans 8:29 correctly, God's design for us from the beginning of creation is for each of us to become like Jesus. Yet to arrive at that place of perfection, or as Paul states earlier in that great eighth chapter of Romans, to become "the manifested sons of God" entails a great deal of finish work. Finishing is a tedious and painful process, brought about by the One who is the "author and finisher" of our faith. In carpentry, the finish work is accomplished by a man with sandpaper, steel wool, and a sharp chisel. Since most of us simply don't want to submit to that kind of irritation—the kind that shapes us into the image of Jesus—we do everything we can to escape it.

Criticism is one of God's finest shaping tools. In the hands of an expert it can rapidly transform us from self-centered individuals into people who live and act like Jesus. But since most of us have failed to realize that all criticism, like all authority, is valid only because God allows it, then we run from the man (or woman) coming down the sidewalk with sandpaper, steel wool, and a sharp chisel. It's difficult to understand, but God just may have sent that Philistine to polish you until you reflect Jesus.

When I stood up before that women's group and made that stupid announcement—that I had become immune to criticism—it was the same as saying I no longer had a need to be shaped by God. As a result, I laid myself wide open to a full-fledged midterm exam by God to see if I really was who I said I was.

The test started when I left the luncheon and stopped by the post office before going home. In my box was a letter from Carey Moore, the managing editor of *Logos Journal*. At that time I was still writing the editorials for the magazine, as well as my column "The Last Word." In the envelope was a note from Carey which was paper-clipped to another letter.

"This letter from an irate reader was in today's mail," Carey wrote. "I thought you might want to see it since we'll probably use it in our 'Letters to the Editor' section."

The letter was addressed to Carey and marked "Personal."

It should have been marked "Poison!"

The fellow was really taking me to task for an editorial in the last issue. "Buckingham is so fearful of offending that he isn't worth wasting paper on. . . . Buckingham is intimidated. He's waffling. He's lost his salt. Look for a replacement that can tell it like it is."

I stood at the table in the post office reading the letter and felt my heart begin to race. I thought back on the editorial I had written. I had worked on it for almost a week, trying to say what I wanted to say without sounding judgmental. Yet I realized I had not said all I really felt. Perhaps I should have taken a harder stand. The world was waiting for a clear sound from the trumpet and all I had given them was a slobbery fizzle, the flabbery sound of air escaping from a punctured tire. I read and reread the letter. "Fearful . . . intimidated . . . waffling. . . ." I felt the old depression coming on. I glanced around to see if anyone had seen me standing there, white-lipped, hands shaking. I thought back to the statement I had made less than an hour ago, that I had become immune to the sharp edge of criticism. God, how I wished I hadn't said that.

But it wasn't over. In fact, it was just beginning.

That evening, while I was sitting in my study trying to pen some kind of witty, sarcastic answer to the fellow who had written saying I had lost my salt, Jackie called from downstairs.

"Honey, can you get the phone?"

I shouted back, "I'm in the middle of something. See if they can call back."

Moments later Jackie appeared at the door of my studio. "I think you better take this one *now*."

Just the way she said "now" caused sweat to break out in the palms of my hands.

"Who—?"

"I don't know who she is, but she's *very* angry over something. She demands to talk to MISTER Buckingham."

"Can't you handle it?" I said, trying to hide the nervousness in my voice.

"I thought you told all those women you were immune to criticism," she said. "Now's a good time to find out."

I didn't have the heart to tell her about the letter—that I had already failed the first test. I left my desk and went to the phone.

It was all I feared. It had to do with an article I had written for our church newspaper, *The Trumpet*. "I can't believe you wrote that," the woman said with terse, clipped words. "I've been coming to church to hear you for three years. Up until now I have never been ashamed to ask my friends to come with me. But I don't see how I can ever come back, much less ask anyone to come with me. If you can write garbage like that, stuff that I'm ashamed for my own husband to read—"

I tried to explain what I had meant in the article. That I didn't have much space to say it in, and, besides, my secretary had changed a few words—

None of the old excuses worked. She just bore in on me.

I could feel my eyes dilating as she talked, and I had to work to pull air into my lungs. She went on to say how ashamed she was of me, ashamed to be associated with a man like me who wrote such trashy stuff in the name of Jesus. She was notifying all her friends that my opinions were certainly not hers.

The conversation was over when she slammed down the receiver on the other end with some kind of doomsday threat on filthy, insensitive creatures like me who paraded around in a shepherd's costume when actually I was a wolf preying on the flock. I was so devastated I couldn't move from the place beside the phone.

"Kinda got to you, didn't she?" Jackie asked, when she came back in the room.

I just gulped. Then gulped again. I had a feeling my heart was about to stop beating.

I headed for the refrigerator.

"You don't need all that ice cream," Jackie said. "Why don't you just face up to the fact you can't please everybody. If you keep eating all that junk food every time someone criticizes you, you'll be so big you won't be able to get out of the house. If you're going to react, why not do it with a stick of celery."

Something inside me snapped. I slammed the refrigerator door so hard the entire box rocked back against the wall. Turning to Jackie, I said in clipped tones, "I may have to take all that junk from a lot of other sick women who call and put curses on me, but I don't have to take it from you."

She backed out of the kitchen. "Wow! I didn't know a little ice cream meant so much to you. Go ahead. Eat it all. I'd rather have you like a balloon than Jack the Ripper."

The anger passed, but the depression remained. I

didn't sleep much that night. Half the time was spent thinking up answers to my critic—sharp, pungent answers. Things I wished I had said and would surely say if she ever called back. The rest of the time was spent wishing I hadn't made that statement at the women's meeting. Somehow, everything seemed to go back to that.

Saturday was relatively calm. By Saturday night I was pretty well in control again, only I dreaded going to church Sunday morning and running the risk of meeting that angry woman face-to-face. However, from the tone of her conversation I had a feeling she would not be there—perhaps would never be there again—which was something of a consolation.

Early Sunday morning the doorbell rang. New neighbors had moved across the street from us the week before. Jackie and I planned to stop by but had not had the chance. Besides, the children had reported the man had already warned them to stay out of his yard or he'd call the police. Now here he was, at 7:00 A.M. on Sunday morning, standing at my front door, his eyes smoldering in fury.

"Your cat attacked our kitty last night," he said through clenched teeth.

I glanced out in the carport. There was our gray tabby, Mrs. Robinson, innocently licking her paws.

"But I just let her out of the house," I stammered. "She has been inside all night long."

The fellow didn't seem to have even heard me. There he was, unshaven. Hair mussed from sleep (or lack of it). Dressed in a bathrobe pulled over blue jeans and a T-shirt, glaring at me. "We've lived in neighborhoods like this before," he snarled. "Everyone lets their children and their animals run loose. Our kitty had to hide in the garage to get away from your vicious cat. I'll tell you once, just once. If I ever see her in our yard again I'll sue your pants off."

He turned and started to stalk away. Then wheeled back. "And that goes for your kids, too."

Ten years ago I would have known exactly how to handle a situation like that, especially since I outweighed him by twenty-five pounds. But as a Christian I knew that beating him to a bloody pulp would never glorify God, nor would it help transform me into the image of Christ. So, instead of following him down the sidewalk, spinning him around, and smashing my fist into his mouth, I did the godly thing. I slammed the door with all my might, turned back into the living room, and kicked the nearest soft thing I could find—which happened to be a huge beanbag chair. Unfortunately, the old zipper popped open and little styrofoam pellets flew everywhere.

I headed toward the refrigerator.

To top it all off, that morning when I came to the platform, someone had taped a picture on the top of the pulpit. It was a cartoon drawing of a huge, fat man. His stomach was pushing at the buttons of his shirt, stretching the cloth to the ripping point. His fat fingers extended beyond his sleeves like corn cobs poking from a scarecrow's coat. However, his head was missing. In its place someone had cut a picture of my head from some magazine and pasted it atop the body of this grotesque caricature. Underneath, in letters which had been individually clipped from newspaper headlines and pasted in uneven rows, it said, "HATH GOD NOT SAID, THOU SHALT NOT EAT MASHED POTATOES?"

I looked out over the sea of faces. It could have been any

one of them. It could have been all of them. Or, it could have been none of them. Perhaps it had been placed there by the heavenly being who had stood in the shadows last Friday morning and chuckled when I made my absurd statement about being immune from criticism. Whatever the source, I had learned my lesson. From that time on, I have been careful to differentiate between coping with criticism and being immune to criticism.

3

Take It–and Leave It

Several years ago I became involved with a group known as the Jungle Aviation and Radio Service (JAARS), the flying arm of the Wycliffe Bible Translators. The group is composed of radio technicians who develop and maintain a radio network all over the world, aviation mechanics, and pilots who fly small planes into places like the Amazon jungle, the headhunter territory of the Philippines and the rain forests of Africa. Bernie May, who was then executive director of JAARS, had asked me to write a book about his crew, whom I grew to love and respect as the most daring and adventurous of all God's servants I had ever met. I spent almost two years—off and on—flying with these men into some of the most dangerous places on the surface of the earth, collecting research material for the book called *Into the Glory.*

It was a fun book. A glory book. It was filled with flying stories and miracles. There were stories of planes which ran out of gas over the jungle and had to land on sandbars in crocodile-infested rivers. Stories of missionaries who gave their lives to translate the Bible into the language of the people. Incredible accounts of mighty pentecostal events deep in the South American jungles. It was a difficult book to write, for it included the personal stories of a number of men and women who made up the JAARS team—their trials, defeats, sorrows, heartaches, and victories. In the end I wound up giving away all my royalties. Surely, I thought, if ever a book was to the glory of God, *Into the Glory* was the one.

Then the criticism began to come. Incredibly, some of it was coming from fundamentalist pastors who were disturbed because I had reported several charismatic happenings in the book. I was able to cope with that kind of criticism pretty well, for I knew I was standing on both factual and spiritual ground. However, when I began receiving letters from some of the translators who questioned the accuracy of my reporting, I began to fall apart.

I don't mind being questioned about my theology. That's always up for question, for what man has a final grip on God's truth? But when these dedicated linguists and anthropologists began writing letters, stating I had twisted facts, I got upset.

One translator wrote me from South America. He was disturbed. "In your description of my place, you said there was an ironwood tree beside my house. That's a lie. If you lied about things like that, how can I trust anything else you said." I discovered it actually wasn't an ironwood tree, it was a teak tree.

Another fellow, a dedicated young linguist in the Philippines, wrote of how offended his wife was over my description of the native children. I had described them as

"Indians" when the accurate term is "tribespeople."

Another wrote from Nepal taking exception to my statement that his mission station was at the base of Mt. Everest. While Mt. Everest did tower over his station, and seemed to be just a few miles away, actually he was located a good many miles from the actual base. He conceded that to anyone coming in it looked as if he were at the base of the huge mountain, yet discerning people who visited there knew he was not located right at the base, and therefore would not believe the rest of the book because of this gross inaccuracy. The fact that he had only one visitor every four years didn't seem to enter into his thinking.

After more than twenty-five such letters, criticizing everything from the fact I had referred to a "tribesman" as brown-skinned when actually his skin was the color of chocolate, to the fact I had said the airplane was flying at 130 knots when everyone knew its top speed was 128 knots, I blew up.

I wrote a fiery letter to one of the directors, accusing the entire organization of being "jot and tittle" people who were straining at gnats and swallowing camels. He wrote me back, expressing his own personal appreciation for my work with the organization and his deep approval of the book. Then he added, "When you are translating the Bible, you need 'jot and tittle' people."

I felt like a fool. I wrote Bernie May, apologizing for my reaction to what was, in reality, justified criticism. "I feel my ears getting red every time I think of my 'jot and tittle,' " I wrote. "It's like the time I realized the zipper on my fly had been open throughout the entire service where I was leading the singing, but I didn't discover it until I sat down. I wished I didn't have to think about it. Here I have wanted to build bridges, but I've used a pickax as my tool."

Fortunately, a number of the folks at Wycliffe sensed that I had been miffed beyond my control and wrote me a bunch of nice letters. One of the leaders redeemed the matter best for me. He wrote and said the criticism I had received meant I was being treated as "part of the family," since this close group of dedicated men and women never took time to criticize anyone except those they loved. I let that soak in for a few days and it brought a needed balm to my inner sores.

Criticism from friends is much more difficult to receive than criticism from enemies. If your enemy criticizes you, you can shrug him off. But if it comes from a friend, then it is likely to keep on coming until the matter is settled. Of course, as your circle of friends expands—and as you begin to see your enemies as your friends—this opens you to even more criticism of a continuing nature.

Some criticism, however, is not to be received.

Recently we entertained a man in our home for Sunday dinner who came from a different doctrinal position from most of the people in our church. He had attended the morning service at our church—which by any standard is a "wide open" service. Several days later I received a long letter from him, full of criticism. In his letter he made it plain he would never change his doctrinal position, and accused our church of practicing witchcraft.

"The canon is closed," he wrote dogmatically. "Anyone who says he 'hears voices' today is hearing from Satan. It is simply an occult practice, only you are doing it in the name of Jesus. There is no difference in what you are doing and what witches are doing in communicating with the dead."

It was not difficult to realize he was plastering me with his own inadequacies, his own inability to hear from God—and calling it witchcraft. To equate the "word of knowledge" with "necromancy" is to do the same thing the religious leaders did when they called Jesus demon-possessed. Such criticism is nothing more than the projection of fear. It makes no pretense to transform. It is given only to tear down and disagree. The person who receives this kind of criticism becomes a dumping ground for all those who wander around with their loads of fear, inadequacy, and resentment—looking for someone gullible enough to slop it on. Such criticism is not valid in any fashion, but merely a venting of someone else's fears and frustrations.

Jesus refused to accept such garbage. When the religious leaders accused Him of being possessed by Satan (Mark 3:22), Jesus realized He was not dealing with rational criticism. In fact, it was completely irrational. ("How can Satan cast out Satan?" He asked in dismay at their stupid logic.) Instead of hearing their criticism, He called it what it was: blasphemy. He refused to become a dumping ground for their garbage.

The story is told of a woman who approached Dwight L. Moody after one of his great evangelistic meetings in Chicago.

"Mr. Moody," she said, looking up at the big man through squinted eyes, "I am an English teacher. I am appalled at your grammatical errors. It seems to me if a man knew he was going to speak before this many people he would at least try to use better grammar."

Poor Moody, he did murder the King's English.

Looking down at the little woman, the bearded preacher boomed, "Ma'am, I'm doing the very best for Jesus with what I have." Then he paused, looked at her intently, and added, "Tell me, are you doing the best for Jesus with what you have?"

It was the perfect answer to a critic who had no other motive than to tear down. Moody had learned the secret of taking it—and leaving it.

4

Living Behind a Mask

Criticism from those who have no intention of helping is vastly different from that which comes from our friends—those who genuinely disagree with us. Even though the criticism from friends may be sometimes unjust, sometimes harsh, sometimes irrational, still we must cope with it. We cannot, as with that which comes in the essence of blasphemy, shrug it off as irrelevant and go about our business.

For years I lived behind a fence. It was a fence of my own making. I put it up to protect me. It presented me as having a tough exterior, impervious to criticism. It was all a mask, however; a mask I chose to wear because I didn't know who I was. I was afraid to expose myself to others, afraid they would peel me like an onion and, reaching the middle, find I was hollow.

Somewhere in American literature I remembered reading a story of a fabled New England character who came into town dressed in the finest clothes. Everyone was impressed with his charming exterior. There were only a few who suspected he was not real, but they couldn't put their finger on it. Then one day the dapper fellow was hit by a runaway carriage, knocked down, and run over. Only then did the citizens of the village discover he wasn't real. He was filled with sawdust.

I saw myself in that condition. And afraid someone would discover I was a fraud, faking my way through life, I ran from any kind of confrontation which could reveal me for who I really was.

I grew up on a kind of Sunday school pablum which said unless I was good, God wouldn't love me. I recall, as a child, hearing a primary Sunday school teacher say, "Don't be naughty. If you are naughty, Jesus won't love you."

It took a long time to get that kind of stuff flushed out of my system. Now, of course, I realize He loves me whether I am naughty or not. In fact, the Bible says that while I was still sinning, Christ died for me (Romans 5:8). In other words, He loves naughty kids just as much as He loves good kids; He loves people who steal and commit adultery just as much as those who are simon pure.

That truth, however, did not dawn on me for many years. I knew it in theory, but was never able to appropriate it in fact in my life. Instead, I saw myself. Impure. Immoral. Powerless. Unable to keep the Ten Commandments, much less live by the Sermon on the Mount. Every time I heard a police siren I jumped, figuring someone had finally caught up with me. Anytime I saw a number of cars parked in front of some neighbor's house, I fantasized they were inside talking about me, criticizing me. If I walked into a church meeting and saw a group of people in a tight conversation, I knew immediately they were discussing something about me they didn't like. To cover up, I built my fences. Wore my masks. And did a lot of lying.

When Jesus told His disciples, "You shall know the truth," He coupled it with another spiritual principle: "The truth shall make you free." In other words, if you don't know the truth, if the truth is not in you, then you are in bondage.

That's the way I was. Imprisoned in my own insecurity and fear. I didn't know it at the time, because the falsehood that surrounded me (or lurked within me) also blamed others while it defended me at the same time. Therefore I did not know I was in bondage. In fact, I thought I was free. I thought how good it was to have a quick mind so I could lie myself out of situations. Others had to face all kinds of withering criticism, but I was able to escape it by dodging here and there. Like a boxer who sees a right cross heading his way and turns his head, rolling with the punch and therefore not having to absorb the full force of the blow, so I was able to roll with the criticism. By turning my head, I could let the blows slide off and hit someone else. Sometimes I was able to move so quickly when criticism came my way that I could escape the blows completely. But it was always a matter of dodging—anticipating the next blow and getting out of the way before it hit home.

After a number of years of dealing with human nature as a professional counselor, I became a master at feinting, dodging, and using psychological manipulation to keep from absorbing (or having to cope with) criticism.

One of the first things a counselor learns about human nature is that the negative always comes to the surface first in a counseling situation. If a woman comes for counsel concerning her marital situation, she will—by nature—begin by criticizing her husband. The counselor realizes this is necessary as she cleans herself of all the garbage which has kept her from thinking objectively—or even kept her from hearing from God. She will list her husband's faults, often with anger and hurt. But if the counselor is skilled at his task, he will then be able to move her from the negative to the positive. Perhaps he will bridge this with a statement such as this:

"But he's not *all* bad, is he?"

Then the wife, if she has gotten enough resentment out of the way, may respond, "No. He's a fine carpenter." Or, "Of course he's not all bad. I know he loves the children, but—" Then she may slip back into her fault-finding. But at least she has broken the negative pattern and allowed the counselor to realize that by careful manipulation of his questions he can hopefully bring her to a point of positive resolution.

Or, he may use negative psychology to bring her to the same point.

"Your husband is the cruelest man I've ever heard of. He needs to be locked up."

To which the wife might respond, in anger: "What right do you have to talk about him that way? All you know is what I've told you. He's got a lot of good points."

The counselor will then lean back and say, "Oh?"

Either procedure is legitimate if it helps the woman cope with her problem. However, by using these techniques the counselor is able to escape emotional entanglement and is thus able to move on to the next client.

Many people, especially those in spiritual and professional leadership, are able to deal with criticism by using the same techniques. They realize the initial criticism is usually negative and by remaining objective and carefully manipulating the critic, they can often bring him to a positive point of view.

However, this is simply using a psychological technique to dodge the issue—and does not really cope with it in the true sense of honest receiving.

For a number of years I used this same technique to fend off my critics. A typical conversation went something like this:

> **HER:** You've been promising us for six weeks you would come by the house and talk to us about our problems. Either you're too busy for your own good or you're the biggest liar I've ever met. Frankly, I think you're not only a liar, you really don't care about us. We're not rich or famous so you just put us off. You treat us like dirt.
>
> **ME:** Hey, you know better than that. You're just upset because your house burned down, your five kids are in jail, and Dan is out of work.
>
> **HER:** I'm not upset. I'm just angry. And hurt. You make all those statements in church about loving people, but when it comes down to folks like us who have real problems, you don't care. You hypocrite! You liar!
>
> **ME:** Now, Joyce, I know things are tough. But a lot of other people have problems, too. Yesterday I had to spend all afternoon

with Tom and Sue Jones. The doctor just
told her she has cancer.

HER: Sue has cancer? Oh, I didn't know.

ME: It's really bad.

HER: I feel so bad I bothered you. I didn't know
about Sue.

ME: That's all right, Joyce. We all get upset
sometimes.

HER: Please forgive me for blowing up at you.

By not losing my "cool" and careful manipulation of the
critic, I have successfully kept from coping with a very
real problem: I had not kept my word. The criticism was
valid. Joyce had every right to be upset. But by the time
the conversation was over, I had not only weaseled out of
my responsibility, I had transferred what was rightly my
guilt—to her. She wound up apologizing when it should
have been me.

Dodging, feinting, remaining objective and
"professional," skillfully manipulating—I was able to
escape most confrontations. But it was all a sham. I was
caught in my own little prison, not knowing there was a
better way to face life and its critics.

It's a terribly crowded prison. The world is full of
people who live behind masks. Whether it's at a cocktail
party or a church supper, it's like Hallowe'en. Everyone is
wearing a mask.

A happy mask.

A tough-guy mask.

A nervous-laughter mask.

A swagger mask.

A loud-talk mask.

A strong-silent mask.

An intellectual mask.

A humble mask.

A know-it-all mask.

People are walking around, showing off their masks. Knocking other people down with them. It is a world of utter falsehood. Attack someone who is wearing a mask, poke him with a sharp lance of criticism, and in all likelihood you'll find he is full of sawdust. Or worse, a vacuum.

I put on my own mask when I was fifteen, and kept it there for twenty years. By then my face had begun to grow in the shape of the mask, and even when I took it off I still looked like a fraud. But the more I exposed myself to others, the more I openly faced their criticism, the more I confessed my guilt and admitted my frailties and sins, the more transparent I became. I still have a long way to go, but at least I'm no longer playing the Hallowe'en game.

It began, as well as I can ascertain, when I was in the ninth grade. My soldier brother, Clay, received an appointment to the U.S. Military Academy at West Point. Since he would be wearing a plebe uniform, he cleaned out his closet and hung all his civilian clothes in a bag in the attic of our big house in Florida. It was quite an attic. You reached it through a permanent ladder in my mother's walk-in closet. Going up through a big push-open hinged door, you found yourself in a room as big as the entire house. There were lots of places to play, and lots of places to store things—like my older brother's clothes. Threatening his younger brothers with all sorts of horrible things if we touched his clothes while he was gone, he left for West Point.

On several occasions I crept up the ladder into the attic and sorted through his clothes. Especially was I intrigued by his cream-colored blazer, which was just my size.

That spring my girl friend and I were invited to sing as part of the entertainment for the junior/senior prom at high school. It was a unique honor. Freshman boys in our town just didn't get to attend such events. Two weeks before the prom I asked my mother if I could wear Clay's blazer to the prom. She said no and suggested I wear my corduroy jacket which I had worn to church since I was in the seventh grade. I sized up the situation and put on a mask. Arguing would get me nowhere. It was time for deception.

The afternoon of the prom I went into the attic, wrapped Clay's coat in a paper grocery sack, and hid it in the back of the car. When we got to the dance I sneaked the sack into the washroom, took off my corduroy coat, and appeared on the dance floor in the beautiful cream-colored jacket. I was, in the vernacular of a childhood story, "the grandest tiger in the jungle."

During the course of the evening I spilled some kind of strawberry punch on the front of the coat. Water in the rest room did nothing to get it out. In fact, it made the stain spread. Of course ninth grade kids don't have enough sense to take a coat to the dry cleaners after they mess it up. And even if I had thought of it, I didn't have any money. So after the prom I sneaked it back into the clothes bag in the attic and left it there—hoping, I guess, that the stain would somehow disappear before Clay got home for his summer vacation.

It didn't, of course. In fact, by the time he got home the stain had become permanent and there was a great commotion in the house. Mother called me and my younger brother downstairs, confronted us with the ruined coat, and said, "Which one of you did this?"

I looked over at my younger brother, John, who was about a foot shorter than me. There was no way he could have been guilty. But I could tell by the tone of my mother's voice that she was going to whip the living daylights out of whoever was guilty. Rejection was what I heard, correction was what I was going to get, and protection was what I needed. The only way out of the situation was to confess and get beat up—or lie.

"It wasn't me," I lied.

"Me neither," John said truthfully.

"Maybe Clay did it before he left for school and just forgot about it," I said, trying to confuse the picture.

"Yeah, or maybe it got too hot up there and it just started changing colors," John said, knowing he wasn't guilty but sensing I needed help.

Neither of us got punished, and I came out of the situation feeling pretty smart.

If you want to escape criticism—and punishment—I reasoned, lie when you're caught.

It became easy from then on. When my dad found a dirty magazine in my drawer under the shirts, I said it was something I found in the yard and hid it there so my little brother wouldn't see it and poison his mind. When I made homemade cigarettes out of coffee grounds and in the process of trying to light up while I was driving dad's car on an early morning paper route, hit a fire plug when the burning coffee grounds fell into my lap, it was easy to sa I was really fighting a wasp which had flown in the window. When I went off to college and innocently flushed a bunch of rags down a commode on the third floor and flooded the dormitory, ruining some freshman's entire wardrobe on the second floor and making the ceiling fall in the dining room, it was easy to say, "Not me, Dean Burt."

Especially was it easy when he prefaced his question with a promise to find out who did it and "ship" him. What difference did it make that the entire freshman dormitory was put "on campus" and could not go to town for two weeks—it was better than being publicly humiliated and shipped home.

Later when I was caught in some very serious things—things that break up homes and split churches—I lied rather than face the music. It had become second nature.

That was reactionary lying. I was also involved in active lying. To convince people I was not a failure as a minister, I lied to build my image. Otherwise I would have been criticized. So I talked about how great our church was, how many people attended it, how we were more spiritual than other churches, how many young people we had flocking to the services, what a grand institution we were.

But we weren't. It was all puff. And in the process of lying I was tightening the bonds around me, pulling them tighter and tighter, strangling myself without knowing it.

By the time I was thirty-five, I had been asked to leave two churches, had lost my standing in the denomination, was looked upon as a "fallen brother" by my friends, and had so deeply wounded my wife and children that it was only by the grace of God they were able to stick with me. From being the pastor of one of the largest churches in the state, I had become a nobody, leading a rag-tag group meeting in a tiny little store front with about fifty people showing up for the Sunday services. And still I lied. It was easier than to face the criticism.

Then something happened which brought me face-to-face with reality. One of the families which had stuck with me through all our hardships was Woody and Inez Thompson. Woody's a big man, fifteen years my senior, very soft-spoken. Yet he is a man of unflinching character who sees things in black and white—and is not afraid to voice his conviction. I had a strong feeling he had seen through me, yet I knew he and Inez loved me deeply. I suspected, for the sake of love, they had bent their convictions. (They have since told me they didn't bend their convictions, they just hewed to a higher law—the law of potential. They knew I had problems with the truth, but believed God would somehow straighten me out if they stuck with me long enough.)

The time came, however, when they could stick with me no longer.

In my desire to "be somebody" I had joined the Civil Air Patrol and was appointed chaplain of the local squadron. That meant I could wear a uniform with a major's rank and do a little strutting. I badly needed something to strut about at the time.

The CAP wanted to have a dance and asked if it would be all right to use the church coffee house which we rented in the back of an old abandoned hotel.

"I'm sure the people won't mind," I told the commanding officer. I dreaded leaving the impression we were a narrow-minded group of people. It was bad enough being small. Being narrow was even worse.

"Are you sure it will be all right?" the CO asked. "I don't want to get you into any trouble."

My desire to please won out over my wisdom. "No one will object," I said. I went on to brag about the great group of people who made up our church. Inwardly I hoped none of those who objected to dancing would ever find out.

But they did. Things like stolen coats and lies always catch up with you. Two of the deacons in the church "just happened" to stop by the coffee house the night the CAP had their party. The place was really jumping. Loud music. Lots of kids dancing. They didn't even get out of their car, they just came straight to my house.

"Do you know what's going on down at the coffee house?"

"Er, ah, isn't this the night the ladies have a Bible study?"

"Did you know there's a bunch of kids down there with a live rock 'n' roll combo dancing all over the place?"

"Are they from the church?"

"They've got Civil Air Patrol uniforms on—just like the one you strut around in sometimes."

"Oh, yes, now I remember. They wanted to use the coffee house for a party. But I didn't know they were going to dance—not with a live band. Wow. That's bad stuff. I'll talk to the commanding officer at the next meeting. They really let me down."

The next day several of the men put their heads together. "We think Jamie is lying to us. We think he did authorize it."

Woody and Inez called me the next afternoon. Could I stop by their house that evening. Alone. They had something they wanted to talk to me about.

Woody is a very gentle fellow. When he gets nervous he whispers so you can hardly hear him. I sat in his living room and strained my ears as he whispered. "We are going to leave the church."

"Golly, Woody, we've only got about forty people coming now. If you guys leave, then some of the other folks will leave too. We might as well close up shop."

"Well, I just don't think we can stay."

I could feel my heart pounding in my throat. I'd already failed in two situations. One more would be curtains. If the Thompsons followed through on their threat, it was the end of my ministry. Forever.

"But why, Woody?" I asked.

"Oh, I just don't want to be associated with a pastor who is a liar."

There it was. For the first time in my adult career, someone loved me enough to confront me with the truth. Rather than kick me out, or beat around the bush with incidental charges, this man—who loved me deeply—came boring right in to the heart of my problem. I was a liar. And I lied because I was a coward. I was afraid of criticism.

Woody and Inez had sensed this all along. But they, too, had to reach a stage of desperation before they could confront me with the truth. Now, however, it was out in the open. They had me cold. I could try to lie some more to defend myself, but there was no use. I felt the color draining from my face. The palms of my hands were clammy and moist.

Yet, somehow, it felt good to be so trapped the only way out was honesty. God knows how I had longed for someone to confront me with the truth. How I really needed to be faced with honest criticism, and made to stand up and take it without dodging, weaving, running, or shifting the blame.

I heard Inez's voice from the other side of the room. "If you don't change now, Jamie, you'll never make it. You'll never make it and neither will we."

I left Woody's house and went by to see his son-in-law, Al Reed, one of the young deacons who had stopped by the coffee house earlier in the week. He met me at the door. Where in the past our relationship had been open and friendly, that night it was tense, strained.

"I need to talk with you for a minute," I said.

He gave me a funny look and said, "Sure." But rather than inviting me into the house, he stepped out on the front walk and closed the door behind him. "What do you have to say?"

It was a harsh tone for a fellow I counted as one of my closest friends—one of the few I had left.

"I'd like to weasel out of this," I said. "But there's no way. I lied to you the other night. That's all there is to it. I just plain lied."

"But why?" I could see him softening as the hard lines of anger in his face changed to sadness.

"I couldn't stand the thought of being criticized. I've been so hurt in the past by my own mistakes. And when I made this one I just believed it would be easier to cover it up than to face the music."

It was, to my knowledge, the first time I had made a clean breast of things. The first time I could remember running the risk of exposing myself. The first time I had taken off my mask in front of my friends and said, "Here I am, warts, moles, and deformities. Love me or reject me. I cannot run any longer."

I discovered something that night. I discovered there were a lot of people who really wanted to love me—but they had been unable to get to me because of all those masks I had been wearing. Nearly all of them knew I was imperfect. Most of them knew exactly what my problems were. They knew I was afraid of criticism and they knew I lied to escape it. They knew I was so tender-hearted that I let people walk all over me. But they yearned to forgive me. Only they couldn't, for I had not confessed—at least up until then—that I had done anything which needed forgiving. The moment I began to confess my weaknesses, however, they came rushing in with their love and forgiveness—and for the first time we were able to come together as a family. Sovereignly joined. It has been that way ever since—only the relationship has grown even stronger.

5

Correction and Adjustment

In order to adequately cope with criticism we have to understand ourselves—and why we are unable to cope. This invariably begins with a confession of weakness and need. Yet it is at this point most of us back away. To confess we have a flaw in our character is not only an admission we cannot make it through this world alone (which many see as a sign of weakness), but it opens us to correction and adjustment. This would not be so bad if God did it privately—while we were alone at home or taking a long walk in the woods. But more often than not He does His work through those around us—both friends and enemies. Many times the adjustment comes as a result of our unwillingness to humble ourselves, meaning God has to take more radical means such as public humiliation. Knowing this, most of us tend to shy away from any kind of confession which would result in embarrassment. Yet, in the realm of the spirit, there seems to be no other way. God gives grace to the humble. Thus, if we follow God's directions to "humble ourselves," in order to receive more of His grace—then humiliation seems to be a very necessary part of our spiritual growth.

Back to that onion. I know a lot of people who wear various layers of protective covering. "If I allow someone to start peeling back those layers," a friend once told me, "or if I do it myself, I am afraid I'll get down to the core of my life—and find there is nothing of substance at the center. Deep inside, I know I'm hollow. Empty."

We all have something of an onion syndrome.

I am certain that is the reason I resisted the claim of God on my life for so many years. Even after I surrendered my life to him as my Lord, I still resisted the filling of His Holy Spirit. I knew if I ever came before Him, weeping, saying, "O Lord, come in," that some things would have to go. And there were several things in my life I didn't want to turn loose of.

It was a terrifying experience, as I approached the climax of my life in 1968. I had been asked to leave two churches. My relationship with my wife was so emotionally snarled I didn't see how it could ever be straightened out. She distrusted me—and with great reason. I resented her suspicion, her desperate efforts to hold onto me. My reputation had been destroyed. We had lost first one house, then another. Our furniture—what there was left of it after banging it around from one move to another—was moldering away in a Florida warehouse. We were renting a little house behind the tiny church building, which had been renovated from a child care center. No air conditioning. Jackie and the children were sick most of the time. None of my old friends in the ministry knew what to do with me, so they just stayed away. Only those few folks in Melbourne, who had stuck with us after the last church split, were giving encouragement. And now that they knew me for what I was—a liar, a coward, afraid of confrontations, immoral—well, I suspected it was just a matter of time until they drifted away too.

My only defense was to brag about the way things used to be—or to paint glowing pictures about the way things were going to be. Anything to keep from facing up to the way things actually were. Miserable.

When the Holy Spirit comes in, unholy spirits have to leave. In my case it meant telling Jackie some things about my past—and present—which were keeping us apart. It meant writing some letters to those I had offended—and making special trips to see others. It didn't all happen at once. In fact, several years after the Holy Spirit entered, I finally found courage—and opportunity—to make additional confessions, to peel back additional layers of my onion. I'm still doing some of that, but now it's basically mop-up work. The major exposures are done.

Interestingly, I *was* empty at the core. Not rotten. Just empty. Coming into a salvation relationship with Jesus Christ had changed the rottenness to wholeness. But I was still empty. Only as I confessed was the Holy Spirit able to finish the filling process.

The truth makes us free. But truth is so hard to come by, especially when we get criticized—or rejected—if we speak it.

When is it permissible to tell a lie? Machiavelli approved lying for princes. Nietzsche reserved the privilege of lying for his exceptional hero—the Superman. Emmanuel Kant insisted all lies were immoral—even those told to a murderer to protect an innocent life.

Erasmus had disagreed with this position many years before Kant wrote, but Cardinal Newman said Kant was correct. Instead of lying to the murderer, the cardinal said, we ought to say nothing, knock him down, and call the cops. The Talmud allows for lies for "bed" (inquiries into one's sex life) and "hospitality" (if a host was generous, one could lie about it so the host would not be inundated by unwelcome guests). And, of course, the Bible says no liar will inherit the Kingdom of Heaven.

So, what do we do about the lies we tell? American social psychologist Jerald Jellison estimates that the average American outstrips Pinocchio by telling a whopping two-hundred lies a day, including such things as "white lies" and false excuses, in order to escape criticism. ("I'm sorry I'm late. My wife had a terrible time picking out which dress to wear.")

The fact that lying has become a socially and in some instances legally accepted practice gives us little comfort. Lying by the government—even the president of the United States—has so corrupted politics that the Cambridge Survey Research indicates 69% of the public believe that the country's leaders have consistently lied to them. Lying is now an accepted part of many professions, including law and behavioral sciences. In a typical experiment in social psychology, for instance, a subject is misled about the aims of the study to see how he reacts under pressure.

In medicine, prescribing placebos and lying to patients are commonplace. The requirement for the doctor to be honest with his patient is no longer in the medical oaths and code of ethics and is often ignored, or even frowned upon, by most teachers of medicine.

Journalists often use deceptive methods to uncover

deception. Preachers joke about "ministerial exaggeration," and I know a number of men who are leaders in nationwide ministries who justify their lying to the public by saying, "We can't let them know everything, can we?"

A friend of mine, who had led his nationwide ministry deep into debt, was on the verge of bankruptcy. When I suggested the way to avert further problems and to move back under the blessing of God was to reveal his plight to his debtors, confess he had sinned by not submitting to those around him who advised him not to overextend his credit, and give an honest public evaluation of himself as a proud man who had desired to be a leader in his own kingdom rather than a servant in the Kingdom of God, he shook his head in disagreement. "All you are saying is true," he said, "but I cannot go to the people and tell them that. I just can't."

I understood. I can't stand to be criticized either. It's easier to tell lies.

Yet the Bible says, "If I regard iniquity in my heart, the Lord will not hear me" (Ps. 66:18). Translated literally, that means if I look with approval upon anything which is out of adjustment to the will of God—such as telling a lie to escape criticism—God will not bless me in that area.

I need to come to that realization before I could move on with how to cope with my problem—in this case, my fear of encountering criticism.

How easy it is to explain away the divine commands, to lower the standard of God's expectation for our lives. God does not make suggestions. He proclaims. He commands. He doesn't say, "Why don't you stop stealing," or, "Have you considered it might not be a good idea to steal." Instead, He says bluntly, "Thou shalt not steal," and in the

New Testament, "You who steal—steal no more." That's pretty plain, and I think about it every time I am tempted to slip a motel towel into my suitcase, or walk off an airplane carrying one of their lap blankets. When I regard iniquity in my heart, I effectively shut off my communication and relationship with the Lord.

The other morning the children had left for school and Jackie was downstairs in the kitchen. I had been out late the night before and slept in that morning. I was in the bathroom shaving when the idea came that God had been speaking to me for a long time about some things in my life I didn't want to do. Some of these things are just good, common sense—such as my eating and exercising habits. But I didn't want to do them. Others were far more involved in my emotional and spiritual nature. I started outlining all the reasons why I couldn't when God broke through in my thought process and blocked out everything else, asking, "Do you want my blessing on your life, or do you want to plan your own life?"

Then, without any effort on my part, I suddenly began remembering things in my past—dozens of instances—where I had gone ahead bullheadedly and really messed up things for me and those around me. It was very evident, that morning in front of the mirror with lather on my face, that obedience was better than sacrifice. God was not nearly as interested in my praise as He was in my obedience to the things he had been telling me to do—and not to do. Character was more important than charisma. And at the top of the list of things where I consistently disobeyed was my lying in order to escape criticism.

I dried my face and walked back into the bedroom where I sat on the side of the bed—one sock on and the other in my hand. I thought back to an instance several months before. I was visiting a wealthy friend in a Western state—a man who had been a Christian leader for a number of years. At dinner that night I had listened as he complained about the way a youthful contractor had installed an irrigation system for his pasture. He was displeased with the job and said he was not going to give the young fellow the last payment.

His wife interrupted. "But you promised him full payment when he completed the job."

"That doesn't make any difference," my friend said. "I'm not going to pay for unsatisfactory work. Besides, it wasn't in writing."

I shuddered. Do things have to be in writing for a Christian to feel obligated to keep his word?

After dinner we went into the library to continue our conversation. We had shifted to a different subject—discussing various aspects of the ministry we were promoting, and wondering why God was not blessing as we felt He should—when the phone rang.

It was the young contractor calling about his last payment on the irrigation project. My friend, who had answered the phone, suddenly began speaking with a Mexican accent. I could hardly believe my ears.

"Sorry, señor, Meester Boss not here. He leave early this morning to fly to Sweden. He be gone two, three week. Por favor, you call back some other time. Adios."

I looked over at my friend's wife, who was sitting across the room. She just shrugged her shoulders and held her hands up in a helpless gesture.

I looked back at my friend who was hanging up the phone. "I'll just let him cool his heels for a while," he said.

His wife protested. "But he needs the money."

"Then he should have done the job correctly."

I could keep silent no longer. "Then why didn't you just tell him you were displeased with the job and tell him you weren't going to pay him until he did it right? Why all this charade?"

"Listen," my friend said, "I've got too many incompetent people working around me now. If I try to get involved in all their affairs I'll never be able to finish what God has told me to do."

It was useless to argue. Somehow, though, it eluded him that God's primary task for his life might be straightening out his own character, rather than promoting the charismatic movement.

All that flashed through my mind that morning as I sat on the side of the bed in my undershorts pulling on my socks. I remembered how I had, on at least one occasion, related that story to another friend as a prime example of spiritual inconsistency. But that morning, as I sat there, I realized I was in even worse condition. Not only was I guilty of exactly the same thing—lying to protect myself from confrontation and any resultant criticism—but I had gone one step beyond, and judged my friend by a different standard than I had set up for myself.

The way of God is found in the Bible. So is God's way for us. That is the reason we should be students of the Word. But unfortunately, most of us have spent our time studying things in the Bible we can't do anything about. I have friends who are far more excited about Gog and Magog, about the frogs, seals, and dragons of Revelation, than they are about the Sermon on the Mount. Others have been fighting the battle of Eden for years, traveling across the country lecturing on where Charles Darwin was wrong. Yet in the process they lie, cheat, steal, and have provoked their children to so much wrath they have left home.

I am more concerned about the commands of God for me than I am about the end of the world—or about the beginning of the world. I can't do much about tidal waves, earthquakes, the moon turning to blood, or whether California is going to break off and fall into the sea. But I can do something about my lying, my bitterness toward others, my lack of forgiveness, my overweight, and my unwillingness to laugh.

Sin is lawlessness. Rebellion. It is the arrogant violation of God's will for our lives. God tells us to do things. We don't do them. Our lives fall to pieces. We come running, crying out for help. When we don't receive it, we get mad and storm off with our arrogance and belligerence. Just as proud after we have failed as we were before.

In our failure we turn to a man of God for help. What we want is money, or condolence, or a job. Instead, the man of God says, "Get right with God. Stop doing what is wrong. Start doing what is right." But that's not what we want to hear, so we go around complaining and saying, "I asked for bread and he gave me a stone."

Yet, in the long run, the only help we'll ever find is when we "get right with God." There is no other help. Everything else is putting Band-aids on diabetes sores. Until we get down to the heart of our problem it will continue to recur, and each recurrence brings us nearer death.

That's the reason the Bible commands us to be "filled with the Holy Spirit." The Spirit of God is more than a teacher, He is a purgative—a spiritual laxative—flushing out of our bodies the carnal nature, bringing us to a place of transparency where we are conformed to the image of Christ.

Jesus didn't come to bring glory to himself. He came to bring glory to the Father. He didn't come so men could see Him. He came that men could see the Father. He was so filled with the Holy Spirit that He became transparent. Thus, looking at Jesus we see God in His perfectness, in His beauty, in His holiness, in His maturity, in His power. Jesus was so transparent we are able to look right through Him and see God.

Only the man or woman who has been filled with the Holy Spirit can adequately cope with criticism. Others can make strides in that direction, using their own emotional and mental strength. But eventually they fall back on psychological manipulations to handle the real tough issues—arguing, scoffing, reasoning, ignoring, or adjusting. Only those who are filled with the same Spirit who filled Jesus can ever hope to come to perfect spiritual health. Even with those there are constant setbacks. However, I like to remember something Rufus Moseley wrote in one of his books, *Manifest Victory*: "He who gives himself and all that he has to be led by the Spirit is headed rightly, no matter how imperceptible his progress may be."

6

A Jar Full of Rocks

The "filling" of the Holy Spirit is a process, not an experience. It starts with an experience (sometimes called the baptism of the Holy Spirit) as all processes do. But it continues. Paul's command, "Be ye filled with the Holy Spirit," is actually, in the Greek, a continuing present tense, more accurately translated, "Be ye filled, and filled again, and filled again, and filled again, and filled again, *ad infinitum.*" In the process all the self and ego, all the pride and carnality—all those things which block truth as it tries to get from ear to mouth, from mind to foot—are flushed out by the constant flow of the Holy Spirit. Bit by bit we begin to realize we don't have to lie, exaggerate, pretend, or impress—for our security does not lie in what others think about us, but in who we are before God. That's the reason we do not have to fear criticism. If it is justified, it can only strengthen us. If it is unjustified, it cannot hurt us. We can afford to be ourselves. And others, looking at us and seeing the work of the Spirit in our lives, will glorify the Father which is in heaven.

That's the reason the truth makes you free. It makes you free to be the kind of person God wants you to be—the kind of person you've always wanted to be yourself. When the Bible says God gives you the desires of your heart, that is one of the priority areas—to be the kind of person you always wanted to be. To be uniquely you. Just the way He made you before your life got all fouled up with garbage—reactions, fear, and sin.

I think about this occasionally when I am worshiping God. For years I relegated "worship" to a few moments on Sunday morning—dull, boring moments at that. Then came the experience of the baptism in the Holy Spirit. Gradually, as the Holy Spirit began the process of filling, I became free. Until one day, after resisting for many months any kind of physical demonstration of worship, I lifted one hand to God while I was singing. It seemed so *natural*—to obey Him.

> Because thy steadfast love is better than life, my
> lips will praise thee.
> So will I bless thee as long as I live;
> I will lift up my hands and call upon thy name
> (Ps. 63:3-4 Revised Standard Version).

> I will therefore that men pray every where,
> lifting up holy hands . . .(1 Tim. 2:8 KJV).

I had been taught, since my youth, that the human body was something which needed to be "put down." It was the source of all evil. Once we escaped the body, we could be free. As long as we were encased in this fleshly body, we would always be defeated.

That's not true. We'll never be totally fulfilled here on

earth; but we don't need to walk in defeat. Paul wrote the Philippians:

> In nothing I shall be ashamed, but that with all boldness, as always, so now also Christ shall be magnified in my body, whether it be by life, or by death (Phil. 1:20 KJV).

Earlier he had written the Corinthian church:

> Always bearing about in the body the dying of the Lord Jesus, that the life also of Jesus might be made manifest in our body (2 Cor. 4:10 KJV).

It was a reminder of the earlier admonition:

> For ye are bought with a price: therefore glorify God in your body, and in your spirit, which are God's (1 Cor. 6:20 KJV).

Freedom had been there all along, just misinterpreted to me by well-meaning but misguided teachers who thought anything physical was sinful. So, I raised first one hand to God—and then the other. Since that time my praise has become more and more physical. Sometimes in moments of exaltation I not only raise my hands, but I clap them. Other times, especially when I am singing praise to Him, I cannot keep my feet still. The natural rhythm He has put in my body to respond to music is set free and, flowing with the Holy Spirit, causes me to dance before Him.

Because I have been set free from the old inhibitions which made me a slave to public opinion, I no longer really care if others see me in some of my ridiculous forms of worship. For that's the person I really am. To chain my hands to a hymn book, or nail my feet to the floor, or tell me I cannot cry or laugh in public, would be like putting an eagle in a canary cage.

This same freedom which has released me to praise God with my body—and in doing so release my spirit to praise Him even more— also allows me to recognize that others may not want to join in such exaltation. For that reason I never tell people they have to worship the same way I do. If they want to sit while I am standing, I am delighted. If they want to kneel while I am dancing, I am not offended. If they want to shout while I am bowing in quiet meditation, I rejoice. God has made each of us to be individuals. The truth will not make us puppets, or robots, or paper dolls which all look alike. The truth will make us free. And that's the reason we need to be constantly filled with the Holy Spirit.

Only one person in history has ever been perfectly filled with the Holy Spirit. Jesus, the man who had no sin. The rest of us are "being filled." To say I am "filled with the Spirit" is misleading. What I am actually saying is I have been filled to my present capacity.

It is similar to a jar filled with pebbles—and with water. Depending on what you are looking for, the glass is either filled with pebbles or water. So it is with the life of the Spirit-baptized believer. He is a strange and wonderful mixture of pebbles and water. If some spiritual detective comes along and puts his magnifying glass on this strange man, he will discover all kinds of pebbles. Some round, some square, some sharp, some dull. All are flaws in his nature. All keep him from being transparent. All disqualify him from being perfect.

On the other hand, despite the pebbles in his life, he is also filled with water. You can pick him up and drink—and quench your thirst. You have to be careful, especially in the early days after he has been filled with the Spirit, not to swallow some of his rocks. And quite frankly, sometimes it's better to stay away from one of these mixed-bag Christians. In other words, it may be better to go thirsty than to strangle on some rock he may try to give you along with his water. But the water is pure, and chances are if you shake their container, instead of showering you with rocks and dirt as before, it will slosh the water of the Holy Spirit on you. Don't shake him too hard, at least not for a while, however, or you're liable to get a boulder on your head.

But as the process of the filling of the Holy Spirit continues, there are less rocks and more water. In fact, there are several "continuing present" commands in the Bible besides "be ye filled with the Holy Spirit." Another is "repent, for the kingdom of heaven is at hand." Repentance, therefore, is needed daily. So is confession of sin. "If we confess our sin, he is faithful and just to forgive us our sin and cleanse us from all unrighteousness" (1 John 1:9). Thus we have the picture of a Spirit-baptized man, on a daily basis—through repentance and confession—reaching down into his glass and taking out those pebbles which have broken loose (because of the softening power of the water of the Spirit) from the crusted mass in the bottom of the glass, and exorcising them from his body.

Every time this is done, every time a pebble is removed from the glass, the water level goes down. This calls for constant refilling with the Holy Spirit. Or, as my old Pentecostal friends sometimes sing, "Keep me under the spout where the glory runs out." Once filled, however, it is easier to cope—not only with criticism, but with all of the crises of life.

In the first chapter I said I had worked out a system which is helping me solve my problem—the problem of coping with criticism. It seems that ever since I became a Christian someone has been criticizing me. For the first dozen years of my Christian life I was criticized because I wasn't spiritual enough. In looking back on my life, I realize the criticism was justified. For the last dozen years, since I started filling my jar with water, I have been criticized for being too spiritual, too radical, too enthusiastic, too charismatic, too honest. There are times when I just sit back and shake my head. Thank God I don't have to please everybody. Thank God I don't have to please anybody.

Every book I have written has offended someone— some far more than one.

It was evident that if I didn't learn to cope with criticism I would soon become like Woody Allen, who was afraid to attend the Academy Awards banquet—where he had been nominated to receive an Oscar—for fear they would give it to someone else.

It was about this time these principles began to emerge. These principles, by the way, can be applied to all levels of criticism. How do you react when people make fun of the shape of your nose, giggle when you make grammatical errors, or joke about you because you're going bald? What do you do when you happen on a small cluster of people and hear them talking about the way you discipline (or don't discipline) your kids? What is your reaction when people criticize you for singing off key, doing a poor job, or call you a religious fanatic?

How do you cope with criticism?

In answer to that, I give you a six-part formula.

BOOK TWO

1

Remember Who You Are

It is impossible to separate me from my background. I am not only who I am, I am what I was. My family, my education, my Christian experience, my call, my place in the community—all combine to make me who I am. I am the son of Walter and Elvira Buckingham. I was born and raised in Florida where my father was in the citrus fruit business. I was a fairly good high school athlete. I was active in college politics, was president of my Greek letter fraternity, and was known as a typical BMOC (Big Man On Campus). I married my childhood sweetheart, graduated from a Southern Baptist seminary in Texas, and was a successful pastor of a large church in South Carolina.

All that happened before the bottom fell out of my life. For several years it looked as if there was no hope, ever, for restoration. But since then there have been a number of new experiences with God which have shaped me in a new mold. Many of those old relationships, once so badly shattered, have been wonderfully mended. In a nutshell, things couldn't be better.

Yet I found when I was under fire from some critic I often forgot all that. I reacted like Elijah who had just won the most important battle of the Old Testament, calling down fire from heaven to consume the sacrifice on Mt. Carmel in front of hundreds of pagan priests. This was followed by one of the greatest revivals in history. Yet the very next day he is running for his life, unable to cope with the threats of the angry Queen Jezebel.

I, too, had that tendency to take off into the wilderness, looking for a juniper bush to squat under while I cried out, "O Lord, it is enough. Take away my life."

If Jesus Christ came into the world for no other reason, it was to tell us who we really are, who God intends for us to be, and give us strength to face up to and overcome life's problems.

A lot of people have forgotten who they are. That is the reason they do strange things to themselves and strange things to each other. They have forgotten they are members of the kingdom of God, joint heirs with Jesus Christ.

If you have accepted Jesus Christ as your Savior, then you are a child of the King, a prince in the Kingdom. Nobody can knock that crown off your head. When someone gives you a picture of a huge man with your face pasted on top, you don't have to receive it. All you have to do is look at it and say, "That's not me. The real me is built like Mr. America, has the voice of Bing Crosby, the money of Nelson Rockefeller, and the wisdom of Solomon. All because I am the child of the King." To be sure, when you take off your pajama top in the bathroom and see yourself in the mirror, you may not look like Mr. America. And when you sit down to pay your bills, you may not feel like Nelson Rockefeller. And when your children call you stupid and storm out of the house, you may not think of yourself as Solomon—but the difference between the fool and the wise man is, the wise man is able to see with God's eyes, while the fool sees only with the eyes of man.

It is imperative for us to remember who we are. If someone is ripping your ear off on the telephone and you begin to react, you need to step back and say, "Whoa! That's not who I am. I am a child of the King. A prince in the Kingdom. What business does royalty have getting angry. Or depressed. I need to remember who I am."

Some Greek philosopher—Plato, Pythagoras, Chilo, Thales, or Socrates—suggested words which were later inscribed upon the Delphic oracle: "Know Thyself." I discovered that until I was at least willing to *know myself* I would never really know God's better purpose for my life.

There's a story of a man in one of the Washington offices who went cuckoo. Dashing through the building, he began wildly looking through trash cans, pulling paper out of file drawers, and throwing open closet doors. Finally somebody got hold of him and said, "What in the world are you looking for?"

The man looked at him with a blank stare and said, "I'm looking for me. I'm trying to find myself."

A newspaper reporter, commenting on this, said if he ever went crazy, he hoped it would be in Washington because no one there would know the difference.

There are a lot of people like that who live in cities far removed from Washington, D.C. They have gone crazy looking for themselves. Sad, for God has said, "As many as received him, to them gave he the power to become the sons of God" (John 1:12).

Who are we? David says we're made just a little lower

than the angels, crowned with glory and honor. We are people of dominion over all the earth and over everything that lives on the earth. That's who we are. And when criticism comes our way, we need to step back, straighten up, shake our heads clear, and say, "Nevertheless, I am a child of the King."

As the size of our church fellowship grew in Melbourne, it became necessary for the elders to reevaluate their own capabilities as leaders. Self-inventory was absolutely necessary if they were to remain in leadership capacity.

After a week of thought and prayer, the men came together for an all-day meeting determined to "let it all hang out." We went around the room. Each of the nine men had a chance to speak, telling the rest of us who he thought he really was. Each man brushed aside such questions as "Who do others want me to be?" "What am I doing now?" and "What needs to be done?" They focused on "What do I really want to do? What is the best contribution I can make to the Body of Christ? What are the real desires of my heart? What is God telling me to do with my life?"

It was an interesting and revealing session. Each man got extremely honest. "You guys see me in *this* role, but here is what I would do if I were free from all restraints."

It is a good exercise. In fact, until you begin to ask yourself these questions, you will never find the highest will of God for your life—and will never find your rightful place in the Body of Christ. Neither will you be able to withstand the onslaught of criticism which is constantly being heaped upon you.

A lot of interesting things came to the surface in that

meeting. We found we had asked each other to do certain things in order to fill a need, rather than because that was God's highest will for the individual. We discovered all of us had assumed responsibilities greater than our capabilities, causing numerous problems. One of the men finally put his finger on the problem. "The question," he said, "is what are we willing to quit in order to do the things God is asking us to do."

As I pondered on that, I realized I was constantly struggling with the same problem—how to differentiate between what I *can* do and what I am *supposed* to do.

All of us can do certain things—but are we supposed to?

I learned, long ago, that I could not be criticized for doing things poorly I was not supposed to do, if I never did them. For instance, I'll never be criticized for my job as the driver of the church bus. Someone else may get criticized for backing over a bicycle in the parking lot or burning up the engine for running it without oil, but not me. Why? Because even though I may know how to drive a bus, I'm not going to do it. I can drive it, but I'm not supposed to. Therefore I'll never be criticized for it.

Two weeks after that elders' meeting in which we all got honest, the men withdrew for a two-day retreat in a cabin on the beach. We locked ourselves in and, once more, went around the room. This time, however, instead of saying who we thought we were, we said who we thought each other was. We took each man's self-evaluation and criticized it. It was an extremely painful session.

One man stated he felt he was supposed to be one of the public teachers in the body. All the other men disagreed.

"John, you just don't have it. You do a great job in counseling. But when it comes to standing up before a group and speaking, you don't have the gift of communication. If you only knew how many complaints we have after you've spoken in public. We all feel you should limit yourself to personal ministry, where you are the strongest."

To another of the men we agreed he did a tremendous job leading the public worship. "But," we said, "it's distracting when you can't control your emotions and begin to cry when you sing. If you're going to lead others in worship, you need to exercise self-control, no matter how emotional you feel. Occasionally it may be appropriate, but it's almost gotten out of hand recently."

Several of the men were defensive about their understanding of what they should be doing. But none got angry. And none left depressed. We realized that even though we needed to know who we were, we also needed each other to modify and adjust our own opinions. When each of us fills the role God has for us—and that role is confirmed by men we love and trust—then we will live by positive action to a call rather than reaction to a need.

It is important to realize, of course, that such honesty—facing our critics and even inviting them to tell us what they usually say only to their wives behind our backs—was possible only because these men had entered into a covenant bond of fellowship and friendship. Our relationship was that of a family. It could not be broken by criticism. Thus, we were able to give correction without rejection. Because of this relationship—a confidence in who we were and in each other—the criticism we were receiving, while sometimes painful, was not threatening.

As a teenager, I used to have a recurring dream. I would find myself in a large factory. Everyone was busy, working at machines, spindles, or drills. I knew I was supposed to be there and knew I was supposed to be busy at some job, but I didn't know what it was. Every once in a while the boss would appear and shout at me: "Get to work!" Then he would disappear back into wherever bosses go in dreams, and leave me with a horrible, frustrated, confused feeling. I would begin to run—as I often do in dreams. Up and down aisles of the factory where all the machines were humming, looking for what I was supposed to be doing—but never finding it.

It was a typical dream for a teenage boy who is looking for his life's work. I thought I was supposed to be everything from a medical doctor to a football coach to a forest ranger to the world's greatest lover. In reality I was none of those things. I was just a confused teenager longing to be something other than a confused teenager.

The problem is, I have a friend who told me he was still dreaming a similar dream—at the age of forty-two.

People who don't know who they are will always be frustrated. When criticism comes their way, they will be devastated—striking back, snarling in defensiveness, or withdrawing even deeper into their shell of insecurity. It's not that they think too highly of themselves. Rather they think too cheaply. Christ came into the world to remind us who we are and give us the power to achieve God's ultimate purpose in our lives. The man or woman who understands that will never be knocked down by criticism.

Awhile back I met with a group of ministers who were asking themselves some difficult questions. "Would I stay in the ministry if I didn't have a financial need? Am I in the ministry because I am supposed to be in it, or because my mother (or my wife) pushed me into it?"

It was a hard exercise. Preachers have a tendency to be

a bit pompous sometimes. They wear masks and refuse to let people see who they really are. One man described himself, in a moment of painful revelation, as being "cocky without being confident."

But the sessions were good as each man talked about what he would do with his life if he had all the money and all the freedom necessary to bring it to pass. What would he do if he didn't have to support a family, plan for retirement, fit into a mold designed by some church council, or answer to his bishop. Interestingly, nearly all the men said they would remain in the ministry—but none of them would conduct their ministry as they were now doing it.

Several of the men expressed their frustrations because they were being pressured to assume responsibilities they did not feel God wanted them to do. One man, for instance, said he hated to preach. He really wanted to be an administrator. Another man said he hated administration. He really wanted to spend his time preparing and preaching. Others expressed disgust over being stereotyped as the man who always leads the invocation at Kiwanis or Rotary. At least one liturgical minister expressed a loathing for having to wear a clerical collar—but he did it because his church order (and his bishop) demanded it of him. "If I had my choice," he blurted out, "I'd come to church in a T-shirt and tennis shoes."

These men all seemed to know who they were—they just didn't know how to get from where others had placed them to where they felt they really were supposed to be. And when we left the room they all stopped at the door, picked up their masks, adjusted them into place, and returned to their frustrations. They will continue to run through life and never find their work bench.

There is a fabled story about the famous nineteenth-century preacher, Phillips Brooks. One day Brooks received a letter in the mail. Opening it, he found a clean sheet of paper with only one word written on it: "Fool!"

The next Sunday, Brooks carried the letter into his pulpit in Boston. Holding it up, he announced, "I have received many letters from people who wrote the letter but forgot to sign their name. However, this is the first time I've received a letter from someone who signed his name and forgot to write his letter."

The man or woman who succumbs to the guilt of criticism—both that which is justified and that which is unjustified—is the person who doesn't know who he is, and has forgotten that the same authority God gave to Jesus is ours also.

2

Projecting Love

If you can see your neighbor as yourself—and love him as yourself—then you can see him in the Kingdom of God also. Start by recognizing yourself in the Kingdom. Then it is easier to recognize your neighbor in the Kingdom also. In other words, see him as one for whom Christ died—even if he is threatening to sue because your cat yowls.

Perhaps your critic is simply a voice coming at you over the phone, harsh, bitter, condemning. Instead of allowing your stomach to grow weak, or your knuckles white, view the owner of the voice the way God views him. Then project love toward him. If it is a letter that comes through the mail, picture that person sitting at the desk writing. See his furrowed brow. Look deep into his life over the past few days. See his problems. His inability to comprehend. His deep hurt. Then project love to him. God's love.

The best example of coping with criticism is Jesus on the cross. To be nailed to the cross is the ultimate in rejection and criticism. Jesus received it by looking at His adversaries and seeing them the way they really were—ignorant, afraid, and misinformed.

"Forgive them," He prayed to his Father. "They don't know what they are doing."

Jesus was able to do that because He saw people with the eyes of God. He was simply practicing what He had proclaimed as absolute truth—"Love your neighbor as yourself."

Despite all I have said about the low estate in which we hold ourselves, nevertheless most of us love ourselves far more than we love anyone else. We dress ourselves in nice clothes, spending long hours flipping through the mail order catalogs imagining how we would look dressed in those slinky outfits worn by those gaunt, hollow-cheeked, flat-busted models. We buy ourselves expensive automobiles to ride in. We put ourselves in a comfortable house and spend a great deal of money on home improvements, furniture, carpets, drapes, and various other items of beauty and comfort—all for self. When we are younger we spend countless hours in the bathroom, picking pimples, applying eyeshadow, brushing hair. As we grow older we spend an increasing amount of time in front of mirrors—applying powders to cover wrinkles, lotions to help us look "younger," or wigs and toupees to cover up the real us.

Perhaps we justify this by saying we want to look nice, ride nice, dress nice, or have a comfortable home so that others can enjoy us and enjoy what we have. That is a noble motive—but in most cases it just isn't so. Our primary motive is to please self. Blessing others is secondary. You don't believe this? How much money did you spend last year on a beauty shop or with a hair stylist in comparison to the amount of money you gave someone else with instructions to "get your hair fixed." Or, check the amount of time you spent picking out clothes compared to the amount of time you spent making sure your neighbor was adequately clothed—with the same expensive things you wear. And what about your house? Are you really as concerned about your neighbor's living conditions as you are your own?

To those who feel they have been healed of the egocentric disease which has affected humanity since the time of Adam, I like to ask them the question my friend Bruce Morgan often asks. "Whose picture do you look for first in a group photo when you're in it?"

I've often wondered what would happen if I came into some church on a Sunday morning carrying a huge cardboard box full of money. I imagine myself coming to the platform and announcing that I had just received half a million dollars advance on a book and felt I should distribute it to the members of the church—in packets of five thousand dollars—as far as it would go. I wonder if the first thought of most of the people present wouldn't be, "Praise the Lord, now I can pay off my bills." Or, "Thank you, Jesus, we can finally make a down payment on that house we've been wanting." Of the people crowding down the aisle to get their packet of money as I passed it out from the platform, I wonder if there would be anyone who would say, "We really need it, but the widow Johnson couldn't come this morning—and she needs it far more. Give my share to her. Then if there is any left over, we'll take it."

There are exceptions to selfishness, of course. A friend of mine, Jeff Reynolds, is the son of a wealthy real estate broker in town. His father died several years ago and left him a large inheritance. Jeff has continued to oversee the business, but his real love is acting. After a year in drama school in New York and California, he had landed several outstanding dramatic roles, both in television and in the movies. He still calls Melbourne his home. Although he still keeps an office in the real estate firm, his junior partner actually runs the business.

Over the last several years Jeff has spent a considerable amount of money on dental work—having his teeth straightened even though they seemed to me to be near perfect. One afternoon he called me on the phone and asked if I could have lunch with him the next week. I stopped by his office around noon. His secretary had gone out to the deli to pick up sandwiches and drinks, which were waiting for us when I arrived. Jeff got up and closed the door for privacy and then over his salami on rye he said, "I'm concerned about all this money I'm spending on dental bills."

I shrugged. "How do you escape dental bills? I don't think it makes you any more spiritual to go around with a toothache."

"I don't mean that," he said. "This work I'm having done in my mouth is strictly cosmetic. I really feel called to the acting field, but in movies and television there is an awful lot of close-up camera work. My advisors feel I should look as near perfect as possible. If an actor has a big gap between his teeth, or a terrible overbite, he's classified as cornpone. It's hard for him to get a part in a serious role. If he has an underbite, his best parts are playing villains and vampires. How I look is important. But it's costing me a lot of money."

"Don't you have the money?" I asked, incredulous, for I knew that not only was he a wealthy man, he was making a lot of money on the screen.

He grinned, flashing his white teeth at me. "That's not the problem," he said. "I really want to love my neighbor as myself. That means if I'm going to spend several thousand dollars to get my teeth fixed, I want to do the same for someone else less fortunate."

I put my sandwich on my paper napkin and leaned forward across his desk. He was in earnest, and I suddenly felt I was in the presence of something holy. Very few men take the commands of Christ so seriously. Suddenly the entire room seemed filled with the presence of the Holy Spirit. I could almost sense Jesus standing behind Jeff's chair, His hand on his shoulder.

"I'm in a small prayer group with a young couple in California," he said. "They are in full-time ministry and don't have much money. They both need dental work, a lot of it. Rebecca needs a complete new set of teeth. Loren is almost as bad himself. I could give them the money and tell them to get their teeth fixed, but I'm afraid they'd just turn around and give the money to someone else even less fortunate. Anyway, I don't want to lose my blessing by letting them know I helped them. I want it to be anonymous, so the only person they can thank is Jesus."

I looked up. This time it seemed the figure standing behind Jeff's chair was actually smiling. "I want to give the money to you and let you handle it for me. Is there some way you can get it to them without their knowing where it came from, and make sure they use it to have their teeth fixed?"

I left Jeff's office that day feeling like I had just walked into a warm room on a freezing day. Here was a man who had his spiritual ears screwed on straight. He was not only hearing, he was doing. But as I sat in the car I realized I was getting ready to spend thirty times the amount we had been talking about on a new house for myself. I knew, when the time arose, I too would have to be willing to love my neighbor as myself. Hopefully, I would use the same wisdom Jeff was using, and would not be guilty of throwing God's money down some rat role. But I also knew that never again could I spend money on myself without taking my neighbor into account.

If you love your neighbor as yourself, you can see that person filling his place in the Kingdom the way God sees him. He may not be in yet, or he may be partially in. On the other hand, he may be more in than you are. But only as you look on him with the eyes of love can you see where he is.

Then, when your neighbor criticizes you, you won't be devastated because you see him as God sees him. You'll recognize him as one for whom Christ died. And it will make all the difference in the world.

I'm having to do that with that neighbor across the street who is threatening to sue me because our cat chased his kitty. And I don't even believe it was our cat. I am almost certain it was a big, yellow tomcat who lives behind us. Now there's a mean cat. He not only chases kitties, he chases our Mrs. Robinson. I'm willing to wager he was also the one who chased that kitty into the garage that infamous Saturday night. But, because I am now able (after that first explosion when I almost ripped the door off the hinges) to see my neighbor as one for whom Christ died, and project love toward him, I can smile at him, wave, and call out a cheery good morning when I see him as we leave for work. It makes no difference that he refuses to return my greeting, that he scowls, that he sends messages by the neighbor children that he's going to "get me" if he ever catches my cat over in his yard. That's his problem. All I have to do is love.

Perhaps it's a voice coming at you over the phone, or a letter in the mail. Part of the formula for coping with criticism calls for you to step back and picture that person in your mind. Allow yourself to actually "see" that woman, standing in her kitchen gripping the telephone receiver with white knuckles. Her face blanched with anger. Her pulse shallow and quick, her stomach in knots. She has just finished telling her husband what a no-good bum he is. She has shouted at her children as they went down the walk to school, telling them they were lazy for not making up their beds and threatening them with harsh punishment when they come home from school. As you think about her, you realize that you're fortunate. You can hang up if you need to. But those children have to walk back into that situation—that is, unless they run away. And her husband has to return to her—unless he decides to go home with his secretary instead. Now she is calling you about your children who turned over her garbage cans, or about your dog who decided to do his squatting exercises that morning in her flower bed, or about all that shouting and singing that kept her awake last night because you had a prayer meeting in your den.

Picture her in your mind, pacing back and forth, spewing venom into the telephone, or sitting on the side of her bed gnashing her teeth into the telephone. You see, your problem of coping with criticism is minor compared with her problem in coping with life. Maybe her children are lazy. Maybe her husband is a no-good bum who sits in front of TV all night drinking beer and scattering peanut hulls all over the floor. Maybe her washing machine is broken and her daughter has arrived with two babies in diapers and left them with her while she went to the beach. See her the way God sees her—and project love, God's love and your love, toward her. Suddenly your adversary becomes your friend. Instead of lashing back, you reach out, braving your way through the barrage of criticism, into the empty place of her life—to bring light and comfort.

The Bible says we are predestined by God to be conformed to the image of Jesus Christ. That is God's intention for our life. It is not something we have to struggle to achieve. God has already said, "This is what I have purposed for you."

How is it brought to pass? By being cut all to pieces by this angry housewife because your children have turned over her garbage cans. By being shouted at by a miserable executive because he has nine ulcers and all of them decided to act up at once. By being censured by your supervisor who is filled with demons and can't see anything but the wrong you do. That's how you are whittled down from being made in your own image until you are made into the image of God's Son.

None of us have been criticized to the extent of that early Christian leader, Stephen. Until he took on the yoke of leadership, he seemed to have been an ordinary, acceptable member of the Jewish community. Then he was called upon to testify, and the critics lashed out against him. In the end, their fury was so fierce they dragged him outside the city, took up huge stones, and crushed him. Yet while he was dying, he looked at them and said, "Lord, lay not this sin to their charge." He projected love toward his persecutors. Because of it, two miraculous things happened.

The first had to do with Stephen and God. The ascended Jesus, whom the Bible says "sits at the right hand of God," actually stood up to welcome Stephen into heaven.

> But he, being full of the Holy Ghost, looked up
> steadfastly into heaven and saw the glory of
> God, and Jesus *standing* on the right hand of God
> (Acts 7:55).

The second had to do with Stephen and Saul, one of the persecutors, who consented to his death and stood by watching his murder. Stephen's behavior so affected Saul that he never forgot it. It was the wedge which opened his mind to hear the voice of God on the road to Damascus. For years, long after his name had been changed from Saul to the Apostle Paul, he referred to Stephen's death as the turning point of his life. Stephen's ability to cope with the ultimate of criticism, rejection by murder, was used to evangelize the Gentile world.

It is a lesson all of us, especially those in position not only to be criticized but to be persecuted, need to remember.

Several years ago I teamed up with a Dutch Bible smuggler to make a trip behind the Iron Curtain to Czechoslovakia. As we flew across the Czechoslovak border, I was suddenly aware we had crossed the line into hell. There are few cities in the world where I have actually felt satanic reign and oppression. Prague is one of them. Once described as the show spot of Eastern Europe, it was now drab and dull, filled with long-faced people laboring under the Russian oppression of communism.

Our first night there, my Dutch companion, a young professor from England who taught at the Charles University in Prague, and I drove to a hillside overlooking the city. There, parked beside a deserted road with the windows rolled up, the two men with me discussed changes in the plan to smuggle Christian literature to pastors and church leaders in the nation.

Suddenly our conversation was interrupted by a car that approached up the mountain road. It stopped about fifty yards from us with the parking lights on.

"They are here," the young professor said. "We must go."

He was speaking of the secret police. In communist countries nearly everyone, in a sense, belongs to the secret police. Since the spy system is operated on a system of rewards, either monetary or by giving medals, one never knows when his neighbor, or even a family member, might decide to turn him in for an infraction of the rules.

The Englishman quickly started the car and jammed it in reverse. Heading down the mountain, we roared away from the parking place past the darkened car that held two men. The other car made a sharp U-turn in the road and the chase was on.

"Lord, confuse their minds," my Dutch companion prayed audibly as we careened around mountain curves.

Suddenly our car swerved into a small side road. The driver cut the lights and waited—while the pursuing car sped past and down the street. Then we slowly backed out, turned in the opposite direction, and headed back to the city by a different route.

"Now we can praise the Lord," the professor grinned.

Knowing how many Americans had gone behind the "curtain" and simply disappeared, I needed no other hint. My praise was not only sincere, but like that of the others in the car, quite vocal.

After we let the young professor out of the car—two miles from his home ("I'll walk through the back alleys to keep from being followed," he said)—I thought back on the events earlier in the evening.

The professor, John Montgomery, was a twenty-nine-year-old instructor in languages from London. He spoke nine languages fluently and had been invited by the communist officials at the university to leave his secure position at the University of London to move to Czechoslovakia to teach modern linguistics. What the communists didn't know was that John, an ardent Christian, had been secretly praying for five years that God would provide a means for his going behind the Iron Curtain as a missionary.

The evening we arrived, John arranged for us to slip into one of his "classes" in the basement of the university. More than thirty "students" had gathered in the dimly-lit room. The windows were closed, the shades drawn and the young men and women all spoke in whispers. The "linguistics" class was actually an underground prayer meeting and Bible study.

Each individual in the room had been thoroughly screened to make sure they were not a member of the secret police. Since a recently-passed government edict stated that no groups larger than six could meet for any reason without state approval, each one present was running the risk of arrest and imprisonment if the "class" was raided.

But with the spirit of daring and adventure perhaps much like that of the first-century disciples who met in the catacombs beneath the streets of Rome, these young zealots shared Bible truths and prayed, praising the Lord in whispers.

Following the study there was a time of discussion. As visitors from Holland and America, my companion and I were immediately drawn into the debate. A pretty Czech girl, in her early twenties, was one of the first to ask a question. Her black eyes were sad. Her forehead wrinkled with anxiety as she spoke through the interpreter.

"I hate the Russians. They killed my younger brother and took my father off to prison in Siberia. Every day I see them walking the streets of our beautiful city, and hate wells up in me."

We had drawn our chairs into a tight circle and everyone was sitting, hunched forward, heads toward the middle, so we could speak quietly and yet be heard. I looked up at the intense faces around that circle. Most heads were nodding. They understood. They, too, hated their oppressors.

My Dutch companion squeezed my arm. "They heard me respond to this the last time I was here," he said. "You take it."

"Hate is wrong," I said softly, yet firmly. "The old law said we were to extract justice by taking an eye for an eye and a tooth for a tooth. The new way fulfills that law in one word: 'Thou shalt love thy neighbor as thyself.' "

"I cannot love—not after what they have done," she said, her eyes moist and the lines around her mouth tight.

I reached over and touched her hand. "If you bite and devour one another, take heed that ye be not consumed one of another."

She looked at me intently. "It's easy for you to quote Scripture to me. You are an American. What do you know of oppression such as this?"

"I know nothing of it," I said. "But the one I am quoting

knew even more than you. Imprisoned by the Praetorian Guard and thrown into a Roman prison, he eventually was beheaded for his faith. Yet even in prison he wrote:

> Never avenge yourselves, but leave it to the wrath of God . . . if your enemy is hungry, feed him; if he is thirsty, give him drink . . . do not be overcome by evil, but overcome evil with good . . . bless those who persecute you, bless and do not curse them (Rom. 12:19-21, 14 RSV).

"And what good will it do if I love them," she said. "Will it bring back my brother from the dead? Will it cause the Russians to release my father? Will it change them if I love them?"

They were hard questions. Honest questions. The kind that each of us need to ask—without fear.

"Love doesn't necessarily change things," I said as honestly as I knew. "But it changes you for things. In being obedient to God's Word, you have opened the door for God to directly intervene. You have the power, as a child of God, to bind and loose. Your hate not only binds you—twisting you into emotional and physical knots and bringing sickness and maybe even death—but it binds your enemies. You do not want to bind them, you want to loose them so God can work in their lives. The only way to loose someone else—friend or enemy—is to love them. Therefore in projecting love to them, you set yourself free from the bondage of hate and bitterness, and you set them free to receive the love of God—which changes even the most wicked people into instruments of good."

She had dropped her head while I was speaking. Raising it she looked me once again in the face. Speaking slowly, so her interpreter could translate, she said, "If that word was merely from you, a strange American in our midst, I would spit on you. But I know it is from God. Therefore I accept it." She paused, then reached over, squeezed my hand, and smiled. "And I accept you also, God's messenger."

3

Looking at Your Goal

Criticism, the kind that devastates, often causes us to drop our eyes from our final destination and become entangled with temporal matters along the way. For that reason, it is imperative that every so often—and it is far better to do it when the mind is clear and we are not under attack from some critic—we need to stop and take a look at our goals in life.

The procedure is similar to that used by a private pilot when he files a flight plan for a cross-country trip. He starts by determining where he is. Then he determines where he wants to go. Next he lays out his map on the table and draws lines from where he is to where he wants to go. Then he asks a lot of questions. How long will it take him to get there? Will we have enough fuel or will he have to stop someplace for refueling? Are there obstacles? Restricted zones which he must fly around? Mountains to be watched for? What about radio towers? Next he checks the weather. More questions. Head winds? Cloud layers? Will he have to fly on instruments? Is the equipment all working? How many passengers are going along? What is

his estimated time of arrival?

Once aloft there are continual corrections needed. Compass adjustments. Submission to the air traffic controller who may tell him to go east for a while when he really wants to go north. Watch out for other aircraft. It is a constant process of checking and double-checking—one eye on the instruments, another on the map. One ear listening to the engine and another to the radio. Always keeping in mind that final destination.

The good pilot is constantly reexamining his priorities, always asking himself the question: "Is what I am doing taking me closer to my goal—or farther away?"

I have a small sign above my desk which says: "You are fast becoming what you are going to be."

I know my reaction to criticism is not who I am. But if I let my anger remain, if I grow satisfied with it, or if I become resigned to my depression—then I will become that in the future.

Every six months we need to sit down with paper and pen and list all the attitudes we exhibit when we are criticized. Then on the other side of the paper we should list all the attitudes we ought to exhibit.

Perhaps your list will read like mine used to:

HOW IT IS	HOW IT SHOULD BE
anger	love
hate	joy
resentment	peace
self-righteousness	patience
depression	kindness
fear	goodness
frustration	faith
hurt	gentleness

disappointment   self-control
brashness   gratefulness
false humility   honesty

Now the problem arises in determining how to move from where we are to where we want to be. Start with your last encounter with some critic. Perhaps it came in a committee meeting when you had just finished presenting a project which you had spent long hours preparing. You had run it by your wife and mother—both of whom said it was the finest thing since Bell invented the telephone. Then you brought it to the committee and they looked it over and with hardly a discussion, sneered it under the table. Suddenly you are into your normal reaction—stomach churning, fingers drumming the table, scalp itching, nostrils flaring. You feel anger welling up inside you like Moby Dick rising from the bottom of the sea to crush the Pequod and destroy evil Captain Ahab. You don't want to react that way. You want to react with peace and joy—but you can't help it.

Remember, the problem is not having to face criticism. That is an experience. The problem is how we react to that experience.

Also, the reactions to criticism—or to the critic—are not who we really are. These reactions are but the visible manifestations of some kind of inner sickness. These reactions, of course, are usually visible to other people. Sometimes it is easy to link them to the deeper problem. However, sometimes the visible manifestation is quite deceiving.

Jesus said a good tree brings forth good fruit; but a corrupt tree brings forth evil fruit. Therefore, if the fruit which pops out of your branches when you are under attack is evil, it does not mean you should quickly pull it off. The moment you do, ten other evil bananas will immediately take its place. No, it means you need to change the root system of the tree.

Picture a fruit tree which exhibits a lot of bad fruit. Hanging all over the tree are big squishy things with names like:

worry	immorality
loneliness	drunkenness
insecurity	guilt
fear	argumentation
bad habits	need-to-be-noticed
inordinate debt	nervousness
snobbery	depression

These ugly fruit are right out in the open. Everyone can see them. They are reflected in the way you dress, the kind of music you listen to, the tone of voice you use, your sex habits, your weight, how many times a minute you bat your eyes, your attitudes, your buying habits, even the length of your fingernails. The discerning person easily sees your faults. He knows if you respond to criticism with argumentation, it is probably because you are guilty.

Unfortunately, many Christians have been taught the way to spiritual maturity is to pluck the ugly fruit in your life. Take off your eye makeup, throw away your TV set, lengthen your skirt, stop smoking, rebuke fear, take a Dale Carnegie course and learn how to shake hands, don't worry. But telling a person "don't worry" is like telling a person "stop being poor." It's a senseless statement unless you give him something to replace his worry.

Thus we see our evil fruit on the tree is not the problem.

The problem is the tree itself and, in particular, the root system. Therefore, if you want to change the nature of the fruit, change the root system.

These problems are actually at the source of nearly all our surface problems. When the root issues are resolved, most of the surface problems—those ugly fruit hanging all over your life which squirt rancid juice every time they are plucked by a critic—will wither and disappear. In their place will appear sweet, juicy, attractive fruit—just waiting to be plucked and eaten.

What are some of the root problems?

GREED

Paul tells Timothy that the root of greed extends deep into the lives of most men and women, causing them untold surface problems. "For the love of money," he writes, "is the root of all evil" (2 Tim. 6:10).

Several years ago I had breakfast with two men from a nearby town. They belonged to a small church and were deeply concerned about their pastor. "He teaches submission," they said. "But when it comes to time to submit, he cannot do it himself."

One of the men, whom I have known for years and in whose motives I have confidence, was obviously saddened over the matter. "We are not angry. We do not want to see him leave. But we are confused. He does not seem to be able to love. His sermons are filled with condemnation. Recently he's spent a lot of time preaching on 'last days,' majoring on how the evil people of this world are finally going to 'get their just reward.' "

I recognized the familiar pattern. Fruit pickers are often forced to do a lot of preaching about end times.

Unable to see that real problems lie in the root system, and frustrated by the fact that every time they pull a bad fruit off someone's tree a dozen others appear overnight, they have resorted to saying, "We'll never get things straightened out here, but one of these days Jesus will come with a sword in His hand and cut down everybody who is bad. Goodie, goodie!"

"Have you been to your pastor?" I asked. "Have you tried to talk to him?"

"Several times a week," the men said. "But when we bring up things we are concerned about, he gets defensive—and argumentative. His typical reaction is, 'Well, you don't do it any better. Why criticize me?' "

I decided to probe around the roots. "What do you feel is the root cause of his defensiveness?"

The two men looked at each other. Finally one of them spoke up. "We need to be honest. He has seven years to go before retirement. He has bought a condominium. I—" he paused and looked again at his friend across the table. "In fact, there are a number of us who feel he is protecting himself so he can retire."

The other man spoke up. "We understand that. We want to help him so he can be comfortable in retirement. But we feel his insecurity is based on the fear that if he allows us to get close to him, to see him as he really is, we will reject him."

There are great underlying motives at the base of every life which affect the entire life style of the individual. The love of money—even money on which we plan to retire—is often one of them. Usually we are not even aware these roots exist in our lives. We justify our actions by saying, "All I'm doing is protecting myself," or "If I don't look out for myself nobody else will."

Therefore, to protect himself he builds a wall, a wall which keeps out all intruders, especially those who come with criticism. "The less they know about me," he assumes, "the less they will have to criticize."

I spent some time that morning talking to my two friends about their pastor's basic needs—the same basic needs all men have. One of those needs is a need to be loved. If it is not fulfilled, either because those around him do not love him or because he refuses to be loved, then his subconscious self, where his roots lie, will be forced to seek some other kind of nourishment. Thus greed. Or sexual immorality. Or drunkenness. All of which are simply ways of filling a basic desire to love and be loved.

"Does he know you love him?" I asked the men.

"No, he's afraid of us. He's always been afraid the people might try to get rid of him."

"Do you believe that is the reason he is unwilling to be transparent?"

"Definitely."

"Then I suggest you confront him personally. Start by laying the ground work of love. Since he is operating on a physical level, then meet him on that level of understanding. Buy him a nice gift. Something expensive. Invite him and his wife to your home for dinner. Give him the gift, then tell him—while the mood of love prevails—that you are going to confront him with truth. Do it with your arms around him. If he pulls back defensively, do not let him go. Tell him you love him too much to withhold truth. Remember, however, you are dealing with a pastor who has lived for years with an inner fear that one day his salary will be cut off, that he will approach retirement age with no resource of income. Therefore, make it very plain you are correcting without rejecting."

They did as I suggested. But the pastor was too insecure to handle their love—and their criticism. "If you really loved me," he exploded back in anger, "you'd stop trying to correct me and get behind the program." When they refused to capitulate, he resigned the church in fury, blaming a "faction" who had been trying to get rid of him with finally driving him out. He took a job in the community as a salesman in a shoe store, at half the salary he was being paid by the church, and lived out his life in bitterness. He never was able to see that his critics loved him enough to criticize him. And that had he been able to receive their correction, to cope with their criticism, he could have stayed on in his ministry—in fact, even flourished with the help of good men who longed to stand around him in support and defense—and fulfilled his heart's desire of retiring with honor. But his root of greed was too deep, and rather than face the painful ordeal of pulling it up and running the risk of having to develop a new life style in his later years, he opted to leave the ministry for a salaried job—just to insure his retirement.

BITTERNESS

In writing to the Hebrews, Paul talks about another root which runs deep into our natures, causing our fruit to not only be unattractive, but poison. "Look diligently," he writes, "lest any man fail of the grace of God; lest any root of bitterness spring up and trouble you, and thereby many be defiled" (Heb. 12:15).

Someone has described the "grace of God" as "the desire and the power to do God's will." How do you obtain the grace of God? James says God resists the proud but gives grace to the humble (James 4:6). Therefore we receive the grace of God by humbling ourselves. Since this is a very difficult thing to do, God helps us out by sending humbling experiences into our lives—at which time he also "gives more grace."

Few people seem to understand this principle. Instead of receiving the humbling experiences with thanksgiving and joy, they react with anger, depression, or confusion. That is because their root system is entangled with bitterness.

An engineer friend of mine, who is a chief designer for one of the aeronautical space firms in our area, told me that pride—more than any other single factor—was holding back technical progress in the space industry.

"There is so much rivalry between the industrial competitors," he said, "not to mention interdepartmental rivalry, that many of the really great ideas are scrapped with a typical engineering formula: NIH." NIH, he explained, meant Not Invented Here. If the idea came from a competing company or from some other department, it was often tossed in the trash can as worthless, even though it may have been far superior to the one being presently designed. The root of bitterness, of course, is always at the base of pride.

When Oral Roberts was seeking permission to build his hospital on the campus of the Oral Roberts University Medical School in Tulsa, Oklahoma, several of the state medical boards objected. Oklahoma hospitals weren't filled now, they argued. Why should we allow another one to be built?

The editor of the state's largest denominational newspaper severely criticized Roberts in an editorial for trying to get his hospital built. "If God wants you to help care for sick people," he wrote bitterly, "why don't you buy one of the hospitals already here in Tulsa?"

It was a sneering kind of attack, one really unworthy of the editor of such a distinguished denominational paper. It could have been passed off as simply bigotry, or unjustified criticism, unless the readers knew that only two weeks before the state executive committee of that denomination had ordered the trustees of the denomination's hospitals—and they owned several in the state of Oklahoma—to dispose of their hospitals. There were too many problems in running them, including the recent discovery that the big hospital in Oklahoma City was one of the national centers for sex-change operations.

Knowing this background, one could see the motive for the criticism: envy, which grows out of the root of bitterness. Their own denominational schools were in trouble. ORU was flourishing on a high level. They had failed in operating their hospitals. Oral Roberts was getting ready to build a new one.

So, the editor of the state paper lashed out in anger.

What was Oral Roberts's reaction? When you know who you are and where you are going, you don't stop to answer little people who are too timid to go with you and therefore try to keep you from your goal by pulling you off the mountain. He answered with silence.

For a number of years, until her death in 1976, I worked off and on with Kathryn Kuhlman as a writer. Although Miss Kuhlman was very sensitive to criticism, she never let it deter her from her goal. Instead, she used it to help her get there—always seeming to make the very best out of even the harshest criticism.

Shortly after she went on nationwide television with her weekly program, she received a letter from a public school official in the little town of Iredell, Texas.

"I love you and love your program," he wrote. "It would have been much better, however, if you didn't have to spend so much time tugging at your skirt trying to pull it down over your knees. It was really distracting. Why don't you wear a long dress instead?"

Kathryn read the letter. "You know, he's right," she said to her secretary.

She never wore another street-length dress on her TV program.

A lesser person would have responded with anger, or passed it off as just another senseless remark, or sneered at it with the NIH mentality. But she was not that sort of lesser person. She heard. She coped. She let it help her toward her goal of communicating. All of which was possible because there was no root of bitterness to give a bad taste to everything which came into her life which presented another viewpoint.

SELFISHNESS/PRIDE

One of the reasons we have so much trouble receiving and coping with criticism is our self-centeredness. And while there is a necessity that each of us know "who we are," this is often carried to the extreme of projecting an image that we really aren't. Who among us has not, on the occasion of trying to project a favorable image, found the whole thing has backfired because our "transmitter" was not on the same frequency as the "receivers" around us.

The naturally sweet young lady, who is afraid she will never "catch her man" the way she is, therefore projects a sophisticated image—only to painfully discover she is intimidating the guy she is after because he cannot cope with her unrealistic image.

The salesman, or preacher, who comes across as a

buffoon because he drops names, brags about his exploits or shoves humor down the throats of his audiences without first ascertaining how eager they are to hear all this garbage.

While each individual needs to reach a point at which—knowing who he is—he sets and pursues his goals, this must not be done without due regard for others or even without their help and cooperation. The truly goal-oriented person copes with and builds upon the criticism of others. He is an expert listener, trying to receive help from all around him—even his enemies (who often speak truth in clearer and more precise sentences than his friends). He is able to remain objective when criticism comes his way *because* he knows who he is, and therefore builds upon the criticism of others rather than building walls around himself to keep it out. He is able to say, "Your view of me is more important than my own opinion of myself."

The Apostle Paul gave a great deal of instruction in this area, for he knew as Christians pulled up the root of selfishness, they could move on to abundant living.

> There must be no room for rivalry and personal vanity among you, but you must humbly reckon others better than yourselves. Look to each other's interest and not merely to your own (Phil. 2:3-4 New English Bible).

> Be subject to one another out of reverence for Christ (Eph. 5:21 NEB).

> For if a man imagines himself to be somebody, when he is nothing, he is deluding himself. Each

man should examine his own conduct for himself;
then he can measure his achievement by
comparing himself with himself and not with
anyone else (Gal. 6:3-4 NEB).

Call down blessings on your persecutors—
blessings, not curses. . . . Care as much about
each other as about yourselves. Do not be
haughty, but go about with humble folk. Do not
keep thinking how wise you are. . . . If possible,
so far as it lies with you, live at peace with all
men (Rom. 12:14, 16, 18 NEB).

However, the self-centered person destroys this
balance between self-confidence and submission to
others, between not being intimidated by criticism and
hearing what the critic says, when he lets his
approval-seeking become a *need* rather than a *want*.
Roots of self-centeredness (selfishness) create surface
demands—demands for approval, demands to be loved,
demands to be noticed. All these things are normal until
they are attached to the root of self-centeredness—then
they become needs rather than wants.

The urge to know if we are loved by others, or accepted
by them, is not necessarily tantamount to a need for
approval. Whatever our goals may be, we need all the
tools we can lay our hands on to help us attain them. And
what tool is more important than information? Especially
is this true when our goals involve personal relationship.

I want to know and love my wife (or husband)
with all my heart.
I want to be the right kind of parent to my

children.
I want to live peaceably with all men.
I want to help and encourage my neighbors, loving them as I love myself.
I want to be a good employer to my staff.
I want to be a good employee to my boss.
I want to be the best pastor possible to my people.
I want to live in loving community with my friends.

No goal which involves personal relationships can be achieved unless we are willing to receive information about ourselves—"to see ourselves as others see us," as Robert Burns said—from others. Criticism is the act of receiving information about ourselves from the hands of our friends (and enemies).

Dr. James G. Carr, a management psychologist, points out that a major deterrent to gaining this lies in our own natural reluctance to discover anything about ourselves that is not flattering. When we erect defenses against our own inadequacies—when we try to hide our faults from ourselves and others—we close the doors to a vital source of self-knowledge, and thus deny ourselves the necessity of spiritual growth.

On the other hand, when we cultivate the ability to conquer our fears of rejection, to curb the urge to deny our flaws, and to become more sensitive to the responses we genuinely elicit from others, we actually become more free to go our self-determined way—achieving the goals we feel God has set before us.

Paramount, however, is the concept that more important than achieving our self-determined goal is what we become in the process. In fact, while we may see our goal as some final achievement of a plan, God sees our goal as what we become along the way. Even though we may never actually fulfill that which we set out to do, what we become makes it all worthwhile.

The Bible points out that while our goal may be to fulfill the law, this is best done in loving our neighbor.

> For all the law is fulfilled in one word, even in this; Thou shalt love thy neighbour as thyself (Gal. 5:14 KJV).

But such a concept is foreign to the world, for it means Number Two is more important than Number One. In his book, *Looking Out for Number One,* Robert Ringer captures the entire concept of selfishness and self-centeredness, holding it up as the only way to achieve happiness. In his dedication he writes:

> Dedicated to the hope that somewhere in our universe there exists a civilization where the inhabitants possess sole dominion over their own lives. . . .

That is just about as opposite from the Christian way as anything which has ever been written. Not only does the Christian not have sole dominion over his life, he does not want to have it. He realizes that without God he is powerless. He is like a branch cut from the vine. Not only does he need to be in submission to God, but he needs to be in submission to the Body of Christ on earth—and to the members of that Body in particular. That's a long way from looking out for Number One.

Such self-centeredness and selfishness is always accompanied by pride. God is especially hard on people who are proud. Only when a man humbles himself does he take on the character of Jesus.

TEMPORAL VALUES

Every so often we need to stop and take a self-inventory, asking ourselves, "What are the most cherished things in my life?" Our answers will tell us a great deal about our root system. Are we rooted to temporal values, or eternal values.

A friend of mine says the most cherished thing in his life is his Triumph motorcycle. Another says it is her baby daughter.

Ever since we were awakened by an early morning earth tremor several years ago, I have spent a lot of time thinking about my values. Most Floridians have never experienced an earthquake. However, I had only recently returned from New Guinea where I had gone through a real live, teeth-jarring, road-buckling "guria." To be at home in what I thought was the safest place in the world, my Florida bed, and suddenly hear the sliding glass door chattering like a kid's teeth on a cold morning caused me no little mind-searching.

Aside from the fact that a lot of prophecies were confirmed that night (and a lot more came into being), our family did learn some things from that mini-quake that rocked our house for a few seconds. It forced us to think about the importance of material things. I mean, if you have thirty seconds to get out of your house before it is swallowed up in a yawning chasm, it seems good to give some prior thought to what is really important.

In an after-dinner conference, I allowed our children

Success, reaching our goal, is vitally related to how much grace God gives us. Paul prayed that grace be multiplied to every Christian. How do you get it? By being humbled. Remember, "God resists the proud but gives grace to the humble" (James 4:6). Nothing humbles us quicker than coming face to face with some critic who not only knows all our faults and flaws, but speaks about them in public. Yet it is this very experience that God uses to break our pride and give us grace.

If you are moving forward—toward this prize of the high calling of God in Jesus—then you are not going to be side-tracked by some minor disturbance such as criticism. The president-elect of the United States, on his way to his inauguration, is not going to be bothered by some angry person standing on the street corner shouting hate slogans or waving a placard calling him a fraud.

I used to be disturbed when people criticized my children and the way they act. That no longer bothers me, for I know they are on their way to something better. So is my wife. And, praise God, so am I. I no longer look at who we used to be. Nor do I keep my attention on who we are. Now I am trying to keep my eyes on who we are becoming in Jesus Christ.

My friend Bernie May recently returned from the Sepik River valley in eastern Papua, New Guinea—one of the most remote places on earth. He was there to visit missionaries and Bible translators who work with aboriginal people. The Sepik people have never worn clothes, so they welcomed a box of used garments from the States. Especially were they impressed with the T-shirts, many of which had slogans stenciled on them.

Bernie said it was sort of funny to see some tribesman running around with a T-shirt that said "UCLA" or "Indiana State" or "Goodyear Mufflers." The women, he said, especially enjoyed the brassieres. However, most of them were not too keen about giving up their braless/topless state, so they fastened the bras around their waists. The "cups" made ideal pockets to carry nuts, trinkets, and small items.

One fellow showed up at a church meeting with his undershorts on the outside of his long pants. When Bernie inquired about it, someone told him it was stupid to wear them under your pants—then no one would know you had them on.

Bernie said he remembered a friend who recently had thrown away his TV and then testified about it in church. Some Christians, the man said, were satisfied to give up smoking. He was going all the way, though, and giving up TV, too.

I guess, if you're going to be holy, you need to wear your underwear on the outside so folks will know you have them on.

The last morning Bernie was in the village, which is about 110 miles upstream from the last jungle airstrip, Ambunti, he rose early. Coming out of his hut he was suddenly face to face with a huge, grinning black tribesman who could speak no English. He was just one step removed from cannibalism, with sticks in his beard, feathers in his bushy hair, and a sharp bone through his nose. He was wearing a T-shirt, and absolutely nothing else. Stenciled across the front of the shirt was: "God isn't through with me yet."

Bernie said he really wanted to get the shirt and bring it back for me to wear. Somehow, it seemed to fit my particular place in life. However, the fellow was bigger than Bernie; besides that, he had filed his teeth to a sharp point and was carrying a spear. I guess the next best thing I can do is have Jackie stencil the same slogan across the back of my undershorts. That way folks can recognize me the next time I stand up to testify about all the progress I've made.

Incidentally, when Bernie returned and told this little story before a group of anthropologists and linguists, they failed to find it funny. They severely criticized him for "laughing" at the tribespeople—not realizing he was really laughing at himself. I guess if you are afraid someone might, one day, poke fun at your faults, the safest thing to do is outlaw laughter. At least it's a lot easier than looking at yourself.

Someone has said the largest room in the world is the room for improvement. When we recognize that, when we see ourselves in the middle of the room and know our goal is to fill it by being conformed to the image of Jesus Christ (and not necessarily by testifying about how much spiritual progress we made or how holy we've become by getting rid of something we never should have had in the first place)—then we're on the way to coping with criticism.

For a number of years we had, living in our house, a big red and white collie named Randy. During his later years he grew lethargic and spent most of the day lying on the kitchen floor directly in front of the refrigerator. We never understood just why he chose that place. One friend, a refrigerator repairman, suggested it was the warm air which blew from the fan and exhausted under the front edge of the refrigerator. I never did buy that theory. I figured he chose that place because he wanted to be close to the refrigerator in case something dropped out. After all, when you reach the human equivalent of ninety-eight years old, you prefer to have your food drop on you instead of having to go after it.

Everything in our house seemed to revolve around Randy. We couldn't take a vacation until we lined up a dog-sitter—because Randy refused to get in the car to go anywhere. Visitors were obliged to step over him when they entered the kitchen, for no amount of coaxing could persuade him to move from his spot in front of the fridge. Even Mrs. Robinson, the cat, could not budge him. One day she stalked through the kitchen, found him blocking the way, and proceeded to walk right over him, deliberately stepping on his face as she crossed his bulky form. He never budged.

When Randy wanted out he would slowly stagger to his feet and walk to the front door. (He never used the back door. That was for children and cats.) He would scratch on the door to draw our attention. If someone did not immediately open the door, he would, in a very dignified way, lift his back leg and wet on the carpet. He would then return to his place in front of the refrigerator. We soon learned that whenever Randy got to his feet, he meant business. He was king of the household because he knew who he was—and knew where he was going.

He was also king of the neighborhood. When we let Randy out the front door, he would walk slowly down the driveway to the middle of the street, turn right, and head for the fireplug on the corner. Head up. Feet padding regally on the asphalt. Big tail waving majestically behind him. He had the unmistakable air of royalty.

His presence in the street was the signal for every little dog in the neighborhood to come dashing out to bark at him. They would stand on the sidewalk, the hair on their backs raised like bristles, yapping in animosity and envy. They all knew Randy was king—and vented their criticism with wrath.

It never fazed him. After visiting the fireplug he would retrace his steps. The little dogs would increase their yapping, but he never even granted them the satisfaction of a sneer. He would walk slowly to the front door, scratch once, enter, and return to his place in front of the refrigerator.

Randy had learned the spiritual principle of dominion—a principle very few Christians have mastered. He knew who he was and refused to settle for anything less. In a world full of yappers, he set his eyes on his purpose and never, until the day he died, allowed himself to be distracted.

Today's saints need to learn from Randy and recognize they are royalty—heirs of God and joint heirs with Christ. The dominion God gave Adam in the Garden of Eden has been literally restored to His saints through Jesus Christ.

For most of us, though, that is a theory which works only until someone—or something—barks from the sidelines. As a result, we can't even reach the fireplug, much less go beyond to the place of peace and provision. There is no need to be distracted by the yappers as long as we know who we are—and where we are going.

4

Face Yourself Honestly

There are two kinds of criticism. And two kinds only. That which is justified. That which is not justified. The wise man knows how to discern between the two. That which is unjustified he passes by, like Randy did the yappers. That which is justified, he receives, realizing it is part of God's design to bring him into the image of Jesus Christ.

The best way to cope with criticism when it approaches is by assuming you are wrong—and the critic right. If you start with the premise that you are right, you will immediately be on the defensive. But if you listen to the critic as though you are wrong, then you will be able to correctly divide the word of truth from the word of error. Often the critic is speaking out of his own hurt, or his own unhealed nature. Many times the majority of his criticism will be unjustified. Yet if you approach the critic determined to let the Holy Spirit adjust you into the image of Jesus Christ, then despite that part of the criticism which comes out of hurt, or that part which is unjustified, you will constantly be looking for any grain of truth in order to move closer to the perfect pattern—Jesus.

Of course, this assumes you want to be corrected when you are wrong, adjusted when you are out of shape. It also assumes that all correction is good—even though all criticism may be a mixture of good and evil. However, into the life of each Christian, if he is being blessed by God, will come one or two critics who are ordained to tell us truth. The critic may be friend—or bitter enemy. His criticism may be full of hatred and resentment, it may be surrounded by his own personal hurt and disappointment, it may spring out of his unhealed, wounded nature, it may be mixed with criticism which is unjustified—but if we are alert to God's method of correction, we will find in nearly all criticism a nugget of truth which we need to apply to our lives. If we are defensive, or skillful at arguing, we'll miss the blessing of adjustment.

When we approach criticism this way, the first question we will always ask ourselves is: "God, what are you trying to say to me?" God spoke to Balaam through his donkey. He spoke to David through the Philistines. If the voice we hear is the braying of some infuriated neighbor, or the saber rattling of a church committee, we need to be alert—believing we need correction and praising God for sending it our way.

In *Risky Living* I spent a lot of time dealing with a particular formula: "When you committed your life to Jesus Christ, you voluntarily surrendered the right to choose or the power to vary the consequences of that decision." In a nutshell, what I was getting at was from the moment you proclaim Jesus Christ as Lord of your life, you relinquish the right to dictate the procedure the Lord wants to use to bring you to maturity. From that time on, everything that happens to you is either caused by God, or used by God, to conform you to the image of God's Son, which is His ultimate goal and purpose for your life.

The only way you will ever hear God's voice through some critic is by opening yourself to honesty. There are a lot of things in my life I am not proud of, things I need to be criticized for. However, in my attempt at personal honesty, I have reached the point—to the best of my knowledge—that no one can criticize or accuse me of something in my past which I have not already confessed. It is the finest defense against the accusers I know. I have, in the past, been criticized by experts. From them I have learned the quickest way to de-horn my enemy is to confess I have sinned. It simply takes all the wind out of their sails. I mean, how can you argue with a man who admits he is wrong?

Whether the criticism is just or unjust is immaterial. Whether you are being accused of something you have done or not done makes no difference. Whether the critic is a liar, a gossip, or just plain dumb does not change the concept. In everything which is thrown at me, I try to ask, "God, what are you saying to me through this?"

God's desire is to incarnate His word in us in this generation. Tribulation is one of the tools He uses, wringing the independence from us, bringing us to a place of weakness where we can no longer play God. Based on Paul's principle in Romans 5:3-5—that peace comes by tribulation—then we can see the critic as our tribulator who is sent by God to help shape us into the image of Christ.

Recently my friend Wylene Hughes called on the

phone. Wylene and her husband, Lonnie, are old friends. We have spent a lot of time together as just friends—building relationships. Wylene is a blunt, no-nonsense redhead who says what she has to say and then abruptly says, "Goodbye." She usually hangs up the phone before I have a chance to get in a last word.

This particular afternoon she called, and I could tell by the sound of her voice she was hurt.

"Have I done something to offend you?" she asked.

"What do you mean, Wylene? I may get angry with you, but it is impossible for you to offend me. You're my sister."

"Okay," she said, "if that's the case, then why—for the last three Sundays when we've passed each other in church—have you refused to speak to me?"

I felt myself getting defensive. "Your skin must be getting thin as you grow older," I joked.

"I'm not joking," she said earnestly, her voice cracking. "Lonnie's noticed it too. You walk right by us. You speak to people all around us, but you never speak to us. Now I want to know what we've done wrong so we can set it right."

I was irritated. Snubbing people just isn't my bag. I felt the old self-righteousness welling up inside. "Listen, you're chasing a wild goose. You don't know the facts. If I've walked by you and not seen you, it's because I'm preoccupied. Not because I don't love you. I don't even speak to Jackie and the children on Sunday mornings."

"Then you are twice wrong," she shot back. "Not only should you speak to them, you should speak to us too. If you're too busy to speak, you're too busy. Goodbye." And she hung up the phone.

People react to criticism in different ways. I have a

friend who gets a twitch in the side of his face when he's under attack. He seems perfectly normal, but whenever he is criticized, his left cheek begins to twitch. The stronger the criticism, the more violent the twitch. One day I had been correcting him about something and the twitch became extremely active. I began to criticize him for that. "Do you know that your left cheek begins to twitch when you're criticized?"

"Well, that's a damn sight better than what I used to do when some knucklehead started in on me," he said. "Back then I'd get a twitch in my right fist and the only way I could make it quit was to bash the fellow in the mouth."

I glanced down at his right hand, and I saw it was in a big fist, twitching back and forth like a cow's tail on a hot July afternoon. I decided it was better not to say anything else about that twitching cheek. In fact, I decided it was better not to say anything about anything for a while. I quickly backed off and changed the subject to something we could agree on.

One of our elders raises his voice when he is defending himself against criticism. Sometimes, even though he isn't aware of it, he is shouting so loud it just drowns out the rest of us.

When I am criticized, my eyes dilate. I can feel them opening up. As a result, I have to squint to keep the light from hurting my pupils. I have tried everything I can think of to bring it under control, but so far I've been unsuccessful. That day, when Wylene said goodbye and hung up on me, I suddenly felt my eyes dilate. I knew I was reacting.

I resisted the urge to slam the receiver back into the wall phone and rip the instrument off the wall. Mustering all the self-control I was given at the moment, I hung up the phone and walked into the front room. There I stood, staring out the window.

"She's right, you know!"

It was that voice, that familiar voice, which often speaks in times like that. I nodded.

"In my sight, you're always wrong. You know that by now, don't you?"

I nodded again.

"But I've forgiven you because I love you. You know that too, I hope."

By this time I was nodding continuously.

"Then why do you get so angry when I send someone along to tell you the truth?"

"But I don't ignore her on purpose," I argued. "I just don't react to people very well when I'm trying to hear from you on Sunday morning."

"Then you're wrong," He said gently. "That's why I had Wylene call."

"What does she know about spiritual things?" I pleaded. "After all, I'm the one who's been to seminary."

But that word "spiritual" kicked something over in my mind. I recalled something I had heard only the week before. I had been in a casual conversation with a theologian from a midwestern seminary. "Almost every time the word 'spiritual' is used in the New Testament," he said, "it refers to our relationships with other people, rather than our relationship with God."

He had quoted Galatians 6:1 to prove his point: "Brethren, if a man be overtaken in a fault, ye which are *spiritual*, restore such an one in the spirit of meekness, considering thyself, lest thou also be tempted."

"Wylene is more *spiritual* than you," the small voice said. "At least she has come to restore you."

116

"Well, she didn't do it in the spirit of meekness."

"That's right. But you don't even talk to your wife and children on Sunday morning." Then He dropped His bombshell. "Sometimes it's far more spiritual to talk to them than it is to talk to me."

Then, as if to cap the entire thing off, God reminded me of that next verse in Galatians 6: "For if a man thinketh himself to be something, when he is nothing, he deceiveth himself."

The wall of self-righteousness is the highest of all prison walls. It locks us in so tight we cannot get out, nor can the love of God get in. Submission breaks down the wall of self-righteousness. By submitting myself to others in the Kingdom, especially to those who love me and speak the truth in love, then I am deliberately taking a jackhammer to the wall of self-righteousness which independence would have me build.

If I always assume myself to be right, it is impossible to receive criticism. All I can do is reject it—either with scorn, anger, or a tch-tch attitude. There is no way to hear from God and receive His ministry through the critics He sends my way, unless I admit I am wrong and need help.

When the founders of Alcoholics Anonymous got together many years ago, they put their finger on one of the basic tenets of inner healing and wholeness. They said the first step to sobriety is to admit life has become *unmanageable.* Until you reach that point, there is no way to receive help. Once you have reached that point, then the door is open for God to pour His Spirit—and instruction—into your life. Often through the critics He sends your way. Then it is up to you to differentiate between conflicts (brought on by God) and consequences (the results of your sins).

If there are but two kinds of criticism—that which is justified and that which is not justified—and if God uses both kinds to teach us spiritual truth and bring us to spiritual maturity, then the process for each person must be different.

This is clearly seen in the story of the two pit experiences in the life of Joseph. The story is found in Genesis 37-42, and begins, as do most problem stories, with the hero's inability to handle spiritual gifts. Joseph was clearly the favorite son of his old father, Jacob. While the older boys had to wander the burning sands of the desert finding grass for the sheep and goats, Joseph stayed back in the oasis where he dreamed dreams of things to come. When he foolishly told his brothers his dreams, they grew angry and plotted to kill him. Fortunately, one of the older brothers intervened and, instead of killing young Joseph, they dropped him into a dry well and later sold him to a slave caravan heading across the northern Sinai to Egypt. Then they took his coat of many colors, dipped it in the blood of a goat, and told old Jacob that Joseph was dead.

God had a purpose for Joseph's life. But He could not use him as long as he strutted. So He had his own brothers drop him into a pit—the Pit of Correction.

Once you are in the Pit of Correction, there is only one way out. You can spend your time rebuking Satan—but Satan didn't put you there. You can praise God, but God does not want praise or sacrifice when you are in disobedience. You can make a positive confession and say you aren't really in the pit. But you are. When you are in the Pit of Correction, don't pray and ask God to anoint your disobedience. Rather, pray you'll fail quickly. That makes it far less painful.

There is but one way out of the Pit of Correction. Repentance.

Much criticism is justified. The critic, either friend or enemy, has spotted something which needs to be changed. God allows him to enter your life and drop you into the Pit of Correction. This pit of justified criticism is God's classroom. Most of His saints have been in it. David was in one when the prophet Nathan rebuked him for his adulterous relationship with Bathsheba. Paul was in one when his ministry so irritated the church in Jerusalem that they took him to Joppa, put him aboard a ship, and sent him back to Tarsus. And John Mark was in one when he was strongly criticized by Paul for being immature—and was left home on Paul's next missionary journey. Much criticism is justified. Only the fool grows angry, depressed, or tries to defend himself. The wise man sits quietly in the bottom of the pit, listening and learning.

There is another type of criticism from which we learn: that which is unjustified. After Joseph arrived in Egypt, he found favor in the house of Potiphar. Although he was still a slave, he was elevated to a position of responsibility. However, when he resisted the seductive invitation of Potiphar's wife, she became highly critical of him, accused him of improprieties, and had him thrown into prison. Once again he was in a pit, only this time it was not because he had strutted, but because he had obeyed God explicitly. This is called the Pit of Curing.

Friends of mine have a smoke house. In it they hang sides of bacon and ham which have been treated with sugar for the purpose of curing. Joseph was thrown into the Pit of Curing because God had a claim on his life—and that claim could not be fulfilled until he was seasoned and cured. Such is the purpose of unjust criticism in the life of the believer.

Jeremiah described us as clay on the potter's wheel—molded and shaped until it conformed to its maker's image. Malachi described us as molten metal heated by a refiner's fire. Here the gold was melted until all the dross and impurities were burned out. So it is with unjust criticism. Joseph had to lose his reputation. The first time it was taken from him by his brothers. The second time he willingly gave it up. He was being tested because God had great things in store for him. He wanted to be sure Joseph would not break under stress.

The Apostle Paul went through a number of similar Pits of Curing. In Lystra he was stoned. At Thessalonica he was run out of town. At Philippi he was thrown into jail. Yet as you read the scriptural account of Paul and Silas in the Philippian jail, you realize they were more "in the Lord" than they were "in jail." In fact, at midnight they were so much "in the Lord" they were singing at the tops of their voices, praising God for this latest rejection.

Their joy, however, was not something which was given. It was something which had grown. A fruit of the Spirit. They were not praising God in order to get out of jail. They were praising God because they had become people of praise—and recognized this unjust criticism as simply part of God's current work in their lives. Praise was not the answer. Praise was simply evidence of work which had already been done in their lives. Like James, they were counting it all joy—not because they had fallen into tribulation, but because they had learned to rejoice in all things, both those which abased and those which caused them to abound. They didn't sing songs in the night to make darkness flee. They sang songs in the night because they had seen the light.

When you come face to face with criticism, be honest enough to discern whether it is the kind brought on by your ineptness—or your obedience; whether you are in the pits of Dothan or the pits of Egypt; the Pit of Correction (justified criticism) or the Pit of Curing (unjustified criticism). Regardless of the source, realize God is using it to shape you into the image of Jesus—for no criticism can come into the life of the believer except as it first comes through God.

There is never a time when we outgrow spiritual preparation. Several years ago when I was working as the editor of a Christian magazine, I had hired an older woman to come in four hours a day as an assistant editor. She had a wealth of experience as a woman's editor for a large newspaper and later as a section editor for a large woman's magazine. She was now approaching retirement age and needed something to do to keep her busy. She was ideal for the job. However, she let it be known almost as soon as she came to work that she was not the ordinary office girl editor. She had held important positions and was determined to be treated with respect.

Shortly after she came to work the publisher walked through the office, showing an important visitor around, and flippantly introduced this woman as an assistant to the senior editor.

Ten minutes later she was in my office. Her face was white and her lips quivering. I motioned her to sit down and closed the door.

"I've had thirty years experience as an editor," she said with a voice shaking with anger and hurt. "I have edited more newspapers and magazines than your publisher has ever read—that is, if he can read. Now to be humiliated in front of everyone in the office. To be called an 'assistant.' At least he could have referred to me as an 'associate.' "

I walked around the desk to where she was sitting, her eyes filled with tears. Her hands nervously pulling at her tiny white handkerchief.

"Let me tell you the story of a man who knows what it is like to be at the top of his career, only, at the age of thirty-two, to lose it all."

"Are you talking about yourself?" she asked, looking up with a new softness in her eyes.

"About myself, and about a lot of others. It's the story of a man who one day is everything, and the next day is nothing. Who finally comes to the place of feeding swine while his former associates continue in the big temples of the land. But I look back on that time as the greatest time of my life."

She broke into tears. "But I'm almost ready to retire. He should be finished with the preparation."

"Not as long as there is pride," I said softly.

"I've had to face criticism all my life," she said. "Isn't there some way I can escape it?"

"As long as there is pride, God will send His critics—even those who breeze through the office and humiliate you—to continue the chipping process. When all the pride is gone. When you no longer care what somebody calls you. Then you will be exalted. Only when it finally happens, you won't want it."

She nodded. "I think I understand."

But understanding didn't make the process any easier. The next week, when the senior editor referred to her as "my gal Friday," she went through the same feelings of rejection all over again. Eventually she quit. The harsh sandpaper of criticism—even though it was not meant to be harsh by her associates—was just too much for her sensitive skin.

She's a dear, precious friend, and continues that way until this very day. But like me, she equated criticism with rejection and found it easier to step back than to march on.

For some of us, preparation is a nasty word. But for all of us it is necessary—if we want to achieve our goal.

5

See as God Sees

For a number of years I "coped" with criticism by sneering. "Well, I'll just consider the source." Especially did I use this tactic against book critics who had never written books themselves, against critics of my children who had no children of their own, or critics of my unconventional speaking techniques who had never spoken in public.

It was the same reaction I often had to those who had not been baptized in the Holy Spirit—yet criticized those of us who had. "Humph! What do they know about it? What makes them experts on an experience they've never had themselves?" And so I would write off my critics with a shrug—and a sneer.

Then I remembered something my professor of military science and tactics once said when I was an ROTC officer back in college. We had just come in off the drill field where my marching platoon, "The Pershing Rifles," had just been given a bad grade for their drill performance. The judges were from another school and one of them was a fat little fellow with glasses who couldn't move from "right shoulder arms" to "left shoulder arms" without bouncing his rifle off his huge stomach. To have imagined him at "present arms" was downright ridiculous.

When the PMS&T gave us the results of the judging—a "4" out of a possible score of "10"—I blew up.

"I don't mind being judged as a poor performer," I said angrily. "But I resent the fact that one of the judges probably hasn't seen his knees in seven years except when he fell down walking across the drill field. What does a fat fellow like that know about precision maneuvers?"

The wise old military professor said, "You know, a man doesn't have to be a butcher to tell if a steak tastes good or not."

He was right. Many years later, as I began to investigate why I wasn't able to cope with criticism, I realized one of my problems was caused by spending too much time looking at the critic.

How easy it is to shrug off a person with "He doesn't know what he's talking about," and never come face to face with the criticism as God intends.

If you are going to cope with criticism, you need to look beyond the critic and see if God is trying to speak to you through some very unlikely person.

Earlier I referred to King David, who won more battles than any other king in history. Yet his victories went to his head and eventually he began to believe he was a law unto himself. He lusted after the wife of one of his soldiers, and when he realized he could not claim her for his wife, he sent her husband to the front lines where he would be killed. He then took Bathsheba as his own. God doesn't tolerate that kind of sin in the lives of those He has chosen. After letting David feel like he had gotten away with it, He sent a very unlikely man into his life, a mountain prophet called Nathan. Nathan had been David's friend, a valued man of wisdom in the court. But this time, instead of giving David advice, he turned on him in fury. "The wrath of God is upon you," he said to David with burning eyes and shaking finger.

Instead of a sneer, a shrug, or anger, David looked beyond the man and received the message. The result was Psalm 51, the greatest treatise on repentance and contrition ever written.

Many years later, another prophet of God came to another Jewish king. The situation was similar. King Herod had taken the wife of his brother. But Herod was unable to receive the justified criticism which came from John the Baptist. His way of coping with criticism was to have the critic put to death.

If you fasten your eyes on the one bringing the criticism, you are apt to miss what God is saying. Wisdom, on the other hand, is being able to see as God sees. God does not look upon the outer appearance, but upon the heart.

Last year I spoke at a Full Gospel Business Men's dinner meeting in New Jersey. Following my message there was a period of singing and praise. I was still at the microphone, my eyes closed as I was praying, when suddenly a woman began uttering prophecy. I felt shivers going up and down my spine. It was as though an angel of the Lord was standing out there in the crowd, speaking God's message to the assembly. I wanted to open my eyes and look. What kind of angelic being was out there, delivering such a powerful message? It seemed directed in a very pointed way at me, and some of the problems I was going through. Yet I feared if I opened my eyes, I would be distracted. So I stood, glued to the spot at the podium, drinking in what God was saying.

After the meeting I grabbed one of the men who had been on the platform. "Who delivered that prophecy?"

"Oh," he said, shaking his head. "That was so bad. I kept thinking you would interrupt her and tell her she was out of order. In fact," he said, "I almost came down off the platform to tell her to shut up."

"What?" I could hardly believe my ears. "I thought it was one of the most anointed messages I've ever heard."

"You've got to be kidding," he said, a look of shock on his face. "Didn't you look at her while she was speaking?"

"No," I admitted. "I kept my eyes shut the entire time."

"Well," he said with a knowing look, "if you're ever going to adequately discern between a false prophet and a true prophet, you need to keep your eyes open. Just one look at that woman and you would have known she was a false prophet. She was waving her arms, swaying back and forth, and at times her face was all screwed up in what looked like a demonic mask. She was obviously a false prophet."

"Did you hear what she said?" I asked gently.

I could see his eyes dilating—just like mine. "I didn't have to hear what she was saying," he said defensively. "I saw what she looked like."

"But did you hear what she said?" I asked again.

This time he was adamant. "Not a word," he said. "One look at that contorted face and I didn't want to hear."

He shook his head and turned away, looking, no doubt, for a few friends who would go with him and rebuke the "false prophet" who had spoken so beautifully to my heart. I could not stop him, but I made it a point to find the woman after the service and let her know that despite what anyone else said, I had heard the voice of God through her.

The same principle applies to hearing criticism. Often we need to step back from the critic, close our eyes, and see if God might be saying something to us which we are too deaf to hear.

One of my favorite stories is about two psychiatrists who rode the same elevator to work each morning. One of them got off on the fifth floor. The other went on up to floor nine. Every morning the elevator operator would greet the two doctors as they got on the elevator precisely at 8:58 A.M. And every morning, when he stopped at the fifth floor, the first psychiatrist would turn to the second psychiatrist, spit in his face, and walk off the elevator. The door would close, the second psychiatrist would take out his handkerchief and wipe his face, and without ever saying a word, get off when the door opened at the ninth floor.

This went on every morning, Monday through Friday, for several weeks. Finally the elevator operator could stand it no longer. After watching the first psychiatrist spit on the second one and then get off on floor five, the operator turned to the second doctor, who was wiping his face with his handkerchief.

"Why does he do that?" he almost shouted.

The elevator stopped at floor nine and the door opened. "I don't know," said the second psychiatrist, heading for his office. "That's his problem. Not mine."

I like the story because it rings with spiritual truth. It really is the first psychiatrist's problem. Granted, we might not like to have spit on our face, or nails driven through our hands—but wisdom allows us to look beyond the spit, and leave the spitter in God's hands.

When I was writing *Into the Glory*, I spent some time in the remote jungles on the island of Mindanao in the Philippines. While I was there, I ate lunch one day in the small hut of two spinster American women who had served more than two decades in the jungle translating the Bible into the language of the tribespeople. After lunch I asked them to tell me a little about themselves. It was a fascinating story. Both of the women had given up the privilege of living in a comfortable home in America, marrying their childhood sweethearts, and raising children in order to travel to the untamed, often violent region of Mindanao to translate the Bible to people who had never seen the Word of God.

During the time they were translating the Bible, each of them had had separate experiences with the Holy Spirit. In short, they had been baptized in the Holy Spirit and began to understand all the gifts of the Spirit were valid in their lives and ministry. One of the women belonged to an independent, fundamental church in Oklahoma which taught the gifts of the Spirit were limited to the early church. They believed that anyone who exercised these gifts today—especially the gifts of prophecy, speaking in tongues, interpretation of tongues, or healing—was a heretic and should be disfellowshipped from the church. She knew that when she returned to the States for her next furlough she would have to tell the leaders of her home church what had happened to her. She did not fear this, for the new power of the Holy Spirit had given her a great reservoir of joy and peace, not to mention a tremendous new understanding into the Word and how it was to be translated.

The time came when she came out of the jungle and returned to her home church in Oklahoma. Almost as soon as she arrived, she sought an audience with the pastor and told him everything that had happened to her—how the same Holy Spirit who inspired the Bible had come to her as she was translating it and given her not only deep insight into her translation technique but more love and joy than she had ever known. She had also received spiritual gifts—the same as outlined in 1 Corinthians 12.

The pastor listened politely and then reminded her of a clause in the church constitution which forbade the church from supporting any missionary who believed that way. She nodded. He promised her he would not make the decision himself, but would turn it over to the Missions Committee.

The next afternoon she was called into a meeting of the Missions Committee. These were people who, many years before, had rejoiced when she went forth to the Philippines as a Bible teacher. They had prayed for her on a daily basis. They had bragged that she was "their missionary in the Philippines." They had supported her financially. In fact, this church was her only means of financial support.

"We rejoice over the many years you have served out there in the jungle," they told her. "We are thrilled you have almost completed your translation of the New Testament into the language of the tribe where you are working. But now we have no choice but to withdraw all financial support. We love you, but we are bound by our constitution which forbids us to give financial support to those who believe as you now believe."

It was a heartbreaking experience. Not only had they rejected her and her ministry, but—just at the time when she had almost completed her translation of the New Testament—they had cut off her financial support.

Within six months, however, enough money had been supplied for her return to the Philippines. When I asked her where the money came from, she said a few little prayer groups, some individuals back in the States who had heard about her tragic encounter with her home church, and from some of the missionaries in the Philippines. These were supporting her out of their own pockets—even though some of them did not agree with her new doctrinal stance. It was a tremendous testimony of God's provision.

"But what about that church back in Oklahoma?" I asked.

"Oh," she exclaimed, her eyes lighting up, "they are the most wonderful people in the world. Why, the church has just entered into a tremendous new mission program. They have taken on a number of new missionaries, they are growing numerically, their offerings continue to increase. What a great group of people they are."

I could hardly believe my ears. "But don't you feel bitter about the way they treated you?"

She reached across the little split bamboo table and touched my hand with hers. I looked first at it, the fingernails cracked from years of manual labor in the jungle, and then I looked up at her face. She had spent almost as much time in the jungle as she had at home. Her face was bronzed from the sun. It had been years since she'd been to a beauty parlor. But the lines on her face were not worry lines, they were laugh lines, little crinkles which ran out from her eyes and from the corners of her mouth. She squeezed my hand as she spoke, her eyes now moist.

"Bitter? How can I feel bitter? They didn't know what they were doing."

She had been able to do that which very few can do—see as God sees.

My friend Jim Underwood heads up an organization called the National Institute of Christian Financial Planning. Jim and his financial counselors travel across the country holding seminars and conducting personal counseling with Christians who need financial advice. In the process of personal counseling, they often have to criticize a person's life style. For instance, a couple has developed a life style of deficit spending—that is, they always buy on credit and are never able to save anything. Then there is a crisis in their life, perhaps the husband gets demoted, and suddenly they aren't able to pay their bills. At the same time, they are going right ahead with their plans to install a swimming pool—an obvious luxury. Hearing this, the financial counselor has to point out they are not only spending their money unwisely, but they have been building their lives on a style which must be changed. This often brings a violent reaction—especially if the man has been bragging that he is a financial wizard, or if the advice given by the financial counselor is exactly the same thing his wife has been giving him. Sometimes the reaction is so violent the people being counseled even turn on the counselor and blame him for all their problems.

After several years of dealing with people in crisis situations, Jim has developed a formula—which he calls R&R—to help measure Christian maturity. R&R is the time between the Point of Reaction and the Point of Recovery, and it applies to all crisis situations in life. How long does it take you to move from the Point of Reaction which takes place when someone slaps your face, to the Point of Recovery when you turn the other cheek? How long does it take for you to move from the Point of Reaction when you discover something tragic has happened, to the Point of Recovery when you begin praising God with all your heart? How long does it take you to move from the Point of Reaction when you hear someone has wronged you, to the Point of Recovery when you forgive? How long does it take you to move from the Point of Reaction when someone criticizes you for something you have done wrong, to the Point of Recovery when you accept the criticism without rejecting the critic?

The closer these two points become, the more mature you are.

In some groups there is a high level of honesty. We have a number of home churches in the larger church in Melbourne. These are "speak-the-truth-in-love" groups, presided over by a home church pastor who is so committed to the group that he will not hurt them by lying to them. The same kind of honesty and transparency exists among the members of the home church. In such groups people are able to sit down and discuss the truth in love. Even though they often react with anger, depression, self-righteousness, or self-justification, they have learned to move rapidly from the Point of Reaction to the Point of Recovery. In some instances where a man might have taken months to forgive a business associate for letting him down, he has now learned to do it in just a week instead. That's drawing R&R closer together.

One night in our home church meeting, a woman said to another woman in the group, "I love you too much to keep silent. If you don't stop trying to push that son of yours into the Kingdom of God, one day he's going to rebel and leave home. I know. Mine did." Before they came into honesty, the woman being criticized would have probably smiled, said thank you, and left the meeting determined never to return. Now, however, because the time between the Point of Reaction and the Point of Recovery had been brought much closer together, she reacted first with anger, but she soon recovered, and with the help of the group moved on to maturity.

Such honesty is rare, even among Christians. But the ability to cope with it when it comes is even more rare. Husbands and wives often find it difficult to move from reaction to recovery without severely damaging one another in the process. But Christian maturity—the ability to see as God sees—moves us closer to our goal of being able to cope with criticism.

Ever since Jim told us about his R&R test, I have been using it to measure my own Christian maturity. So far, on a scale of ten, I'm averaging about four and a half. My biggest problems, I'm discovering, come with those who are closest to me.

Several weeks ago, after an elders' meeting in which the wives were taking part, several of us were standing around our den talking. Jackie really looks forward to gatherings like this—being with people with the same interests, who think as she thinks. It's hard being married to a writer who gets a lot of attention. She has spent the last twenty-four years being "Jamie's wife," and she yearns to have an identity of her own. Thus when the elders and their wives get together at our house—a group of people who don't need to share their sicknesses but can share their health—she thoroughly enjoys it.

On this evening Jackie began a long, involved story about something which had happened to us when we had been on a trip the week before. I stood beside her, fidgeting. I glanced at the others standing around listening. "She's going to take all night with this story," I thought. "And she'll probably miss the real point of it before she's through."

So I waited until she paused for breath and broke in. "What she's trying to say is—" I went ahead with the story, boiling it down and hitting the punch line right on the nose.

Later, after the other folks had gone home, Ray and Wanda Baker lingered. "I need to talk to you," Ray said.

We all went back in the den and sat down. Ray, who is a former seminary professor, didn't mince words. "You know I love you as my brother. I also love Jackie as my sister. You deeply hurt my sister tonight. Don't ever do it again."

It wasn't a threat. Just a straightforward statement of fact.

"What do you mean?" I honestly had no idea.

"Being married to a professional storyteller isn't easy," Ray continued, his face stern. "But has it ever occurred to you that Jackie may want to tell her own story once in a while? Tonight she was doing a good job telling her story. The rest of us were genuinely interested in her viewpoint. But you grew irritated at her and just took the story away—telling it yourself. This time I'm telling you in private. If it ever happens again, and I'm present, I'll interrupt you and publicly correct you."

Five years ago, before we began moving in this kind of honesty, I would have given serious consideration to separating his teeth—but probably settled by smiling and, after he left, quietly determining never to let him

into my life again. I would have also given Jackie an
extremely hard time, not by slapping her around, but by
making her feel like she was to blame for it all. This time,
however, although I could feel my cheeks burning from
the blush (and suspected my eyes were dilating), I
realized he was right—and I was wrong. It took only a
matter of seconds for me to move through the Point of
Reaction to the Point of Recovery. It wasn't the first time
I had stepped on her like that. But by God's grace, it
would be the last. I promised Ray—and Jackie. I graded
myself seven and a half.

Jackie graded me an even ten.

The other night I found myself struggling with one of
those frustrating experiences common to all men who
have married a wife—trying to follow Jackie's directions
in the car when she knew where she wanted me to go, and
I didn't.

Hugh and Linda Evans had invited us to dinner. Hugh,
a real estate developer, had called my secretary and given
her directions to his house. She had typed them out and
handed them to Jackie several days ahead of time.

71 Haven Drive

Off of U.S. 192, one-third mile

west of the Wickham Road intersection.

The instructions were simple. We were to be there at
7:30 P.M. But when we came to the intersection of
Wickham and U.S. 192, Jackie, who was riding in the
front seat beside me, shook her head.

"We need to go east, not west."

I had just gone through a similar experience the week
before when she had a map and was trying to direct me

while I drove. The problem then was, she knew where she was going—but was unable to communicate the message to me. I had gotten angry and in the process of "spinning gravel" had almost wrecked the car.

"Rather than repeat last week's scene," I said evenly, "let's just follow the directions exactly the way they were written."

"All right," Jackie said, holding up the typed sheet of instructions. "But they're wrong."

Like a lot of other people, I tend to think once a thing appears in print, it is absolutely, unchangeably, and totally accurate. "How can anything typed this neatly be wrong?" I asked.

We turned west at the intersection and drove one-third of a mile on U.S. 192. There was no sign of Haven Drive.

"I tell you, it's behind us. The other direction," Jackie argued.

I turned around, went back through the intersection, and drove half a mile beyond. Again, no Haven Drive.

"I told you we should have followed the directions," I said, feeling my pressure beginning to rise. "We're already ten minutes late, and now I've got to go all the way back where I was to begin with."

When Jackie hears the little thing on top of my pressure cooker begin to go "ssst, ssst," she knows not to fiddle with the lid. She said nothing.

I found a place to turn around and roared back out on the highway. Spinning gravel and burning rubber. Back through the intersection, heading west, just like the instructions said. I went a mile this time—and still no Haven Drive.

"It's in the other direction," Jackie's voice came from the darkened navigator's seat.

I could feel the pressure rising. My needle was way over in the red. When I slowed down the big truck behind me blew his air horn. My blood pressure pegged at about 50 psi beyond the area marked "RUN LIKE HELL! EXPLOSION!"

I bounced off the pavement onto the shoulder of the road and tried to get my hand out the window to shake my fist at the truck driver as he roared past, horn blaring. Unfortunately, the window was rolled up and I smashed my knuckles against the glass. Unable to take it out on the truck driver, I turned and screamed at my wife. "JUST GIVE ME THE INSTRUCTIONS, WILL YOU?"

Jackie fumbled in her purse and finally pulled out the typed note. I turned on the overhead light and realized I couldn't read it without my glasses, which I had left at home.

"You'll have to read it to me," I said through gritted teeth.

"But I've already read it to you. Twice," she said.

"Just read it once more—without comment," I said.

She did, even though by this time I had it memorized.

"I tell you, it's in the other direction. These instructions are wrong."

I turned around, once more. "I hope we don't run out of gas driving up and down this highway," I said sarcastically. "I'd hate for you to have to walk to the gas station and carry a five-gallon container back to the car—especially since it's raining."

"Why are you blaming me?" Jackie asked. "I didn't type out the instructions."

"No, but you read them to me. People never get mad at God, you know. They just stone His messengers." Something had happened. I was laughing. My needle was back in the green and the regulator on top of my pressure cooker was silent.

We drove through the intersection and continued east. Six-tenths of a mile later I saw the sign: "Haven Drive." Hugh's house was the fourth one on the right.

At dinner that night as I recounted the story, Hugh apologized. He had been in a hurry when he gave the instructions. Fortunately, my wife knew the way without them.

The interesting factor, however, was how long it had taken me to move from my Point of Reaction to my Point of Recovery. Five years earlier I would not have been able to pass through my anger. I probably would have headed back home—blaming Jackie for the entire episode. This time, despite my flare-up, I moved right through it. In less than ten minutes I was out on the other side of the storm. Even Jackie noticed the difference.

The second test came the following Saturday evening. We seldom go out on Saturday night. It is my one time to keep the calendar clear, staying home to unwind and relax. We wear old clothes, work in the yard, maybe cook out on the patio and eat a lot of junk food.

I was helping Jackie in the kitchen, getting ready to put food on the table for an informal supper. Our fifteen-year-old Sandy, who like her dad has a volatile nature, was sitting at the table reading the want ads in the paper, trying to find someone who was giving away horses.

Suddenly she threw the paper on the table. "Have you any idea how much noise you people make when you chew?" she almost screamed.

I was standing beside her getting ready to put a big bowl of potato chips on the table. "What in the world are you talking about?"

"I can hardly concentrate on the paper," she said. "All I can hear is you and mom eating potato chips. You sound like one of those mulching machines that chop up tree limbs. Chomp! Chomp! Chomp!"

I reached out, put my hand on Sandy's shoulder, and looked over at her mother. Jackie has a pretty short fuse when it comes to lack of parental respect on the part of the children. But this time there was no reaction at all. She was already into recovery.

"I'm sorry, Sandy," she said sincerely, coming around the counter to stand next to me at the table. "I wasn't aware I made noise when I chew."

Realizing she wasn't going to be attacked, Sandy went ahead with her criticism of her parents' chewing habits. "Well, you do. Both of you. And it's not just now. It's all the time—grinding up celery, crushing ice between your teeth, slurping your chili or chomping on potato chips. It's really bad. Sometimes I'm even ashamed to invite my friends to the house at mealtime because I don't want them to hear you two making all that noise when you chew. It's embarrassing."

I looked at Jackie. She was blushing. My own face was burning.

Sandy realized she had hit a tender nerve and reached up and took my hand. "I'm sorry, dad. I don't want to sound mean. But you really do make a lot of noise when you chew."

So the rest of the evening, and ever since for that matter, Jackie and I have been practicing what she calls "the soft chew." It's hard, especially when you're eating corn chips, but we're making progress. Sandy helps us by calling attention to it now and then, looking at us across the table with a pained look and going "Chomp, chomp," when we fall back into our old noisy ways.

Loud chewing, like bad breath and snoring, is one of those things you never realize you have unless you have a critic (or a fifteen-year-old daughter) who loves you enough to tell you.

Very few of us can receive heavy criticism without staggering. There is no way to escape some hurt when we are accused—especially if the accusation is accurate and hits one of our vulnerable spots. It is only when we remember that everything which comes into the life of the Christian is designed by a loving heavenly Father to form us into the image of Jesus Christ that we can find the proper perspective for coping with criticism. Just as all of those in authority are under His control, so He also controls the critics—and their criticism.

That is one of the reasons the Christian needs to stay "prayed up"—walking daily in the Spirit of the Lord. Most of us don't have an opportunity to know ahead of time that criticism is coming. When the old soldiers went into battle they knew almost exactly when the confrontation would take place. So they put on their armor, said their prayers, and went out to meet the enemy. But with criticism, it is likely to come at the most unlikely moments—nearly always catching us unawares. Therefore, spiritual armor needs to be worn at all times so when criticism comes—as it surely will in the life of every Christian—we will not turn tail and run, looking for a rock to hide under. Our feet are already planted on the solid rock of Jesus Christ, and nothing, not even criticism which strips us naked and leaves us exposed for all the world to see, can move us from where we stand.

That's because we're "prayed up" all the time.

Last November my secretary, Laura Watson, and her writer friend, Quin Sherrer, attended a charismatic teaching conference at the Presbyterian conference grounds at Montreat, North Carolina. Both women were wearied by the constant battle of exposure to the world, and they were looking forward to a quiet time of retreat—getting their spiritual batteries recharged.

When they arrived at the conference grounds, however, they discovered that even though they had reserved a room for just the two of them—so they could retreat into the mountain quietness—because of crowded conditions they had been assigned a third roommate: a seventy-six-year-old widow who talked incessantly.

Willing to accept her into their already crowded room, they determined to wait until she went to bed early before they got serious with each other—and with the Lord. They came in that first night after attending the first teaching session and found the older woman already asleep, exhausted, no doubt from her long ride.

"Poor old thing," Quin remarked in a whisper, "she just talked herself to sleep."

They were grateful, however, for they longed for the quiet time for which they had come to the retreat—to pray and commune with God. However, as they settled down in the room for a time of prayer together, they realized the older woman, even though she was asleep, was still talking.

With a sigh of resignation, Laura said, "We might as well go on to sleep. We can't do much concentrating on

God with that going on."

They turned out the light and crawled into their beds. But as the mountain darkness and silence descended upon the room, they became aware of something else. The "muttering" of the older woman—her sleep-talking—was actually intercessory prayer. She was praying in her sleep. Throughout the night she petitioned God in behalf of the conference speakers, praying in beautiful phrases that His message would come through them and bless the people. She prayed for the maids in the hotel, for the girls who worked in the dining hall downstairs, for people back home, for her enemies. She even prayed for Laura and Quin.

The next morning she remembered nothing. But Laura and Quin came away from the conference realizing they had been in the presence of a woman who was literally "prayed up."

Oddly enough, the woman expressed concern that she was so "dry" spiritually. When my friends told her of the beautiful prayers she had prayed through the night, she could hardly believe them. It was a perfect example that you don't have to feel God's presence in order to be in it.

Dr. C.W. Scudder, one of my seminary professors, once told me of spending the night in a mountain cabin with Dr. A.C. Miller, a retired Baptist preacher whose daughter, Clara, incidentally, married my older brother Clay. Dr. Miller was at the time approaching eighty years of age and had gone to sleep early while Dr. Scudder stayed up to work on some papers. About midnight there was a large crash outside the window when a branch fell off a tree and smashed against the side of the cabin bedroom. Dr. Miller, still sound asleep, sat straight up in bed, shouted "GLORY!" at the top of his big voice, and fell back on his pillow to sleep on.

That's the position I covet for myself—and for all others in the Kingdom of God. When some criticism, or some crisis, interrupts my life, I want to be so prayed up that the Point of Reaction and the Point of Recovery are so back-to-back that I will shout "GLORY!"—even in my sleep.

6

The Final Answer

Criticism—even that which is given in love—hurts. It hurts because it demands change. And very few of us have reached the place of spiritual maturity where we welcome change as a way of life. In fact, one of the best ways to measure your spiritual maturity is the amount of pain you feel when you come in contact with a new idea. So, we fight change. We put up defenses which protect us from it. We grow comfortable, sometimes even "set," in our life style. We are not aware we are offensive to others, harsh, cruel, stubborn, opinionated, stiff, and unyielding. We grow so used to ourselves and our way of doing and speaking that any criticism of our life style is viewed as an attack upon something sacred. Thus we react. Often with anger.

When your thumb is hit with a hammer, your body reacts. If the blow is hard enough, your stomach, lungs, mouth, throat—even the fingers that weren't hit—begin to ache and throb. So it is with receiving criticism. If the critic's knife is sharp enough, or if he probes deep enough into your life style, you begin to hurt. It is an automatic reaction.

But the Spirit-filled life is never lived on the basis of reaction. Jesus never reacted to criticism. He always acted upon it instead. Most of us handle criticism fairly well if everything else is in good working order. But if you've had an argument with your wife over the breakfast table, your car broke down on the way to work and some motorist shook his fist at you because you were blocking the entrance to the expressway, you had to push your car two blocks to a service station, you caught your coat in the elevator door and tore off the sleeve, and then your boss was waiting for you when you came in the door because you didn't finish your sales report the day before—you're liable to react. In fact, you're liable to punch your boss in the teeth, turn over a filing cabinet on his desk, and resign your job on the spot.

This, however, is not reacting to your boss's criticism. This is reacting to the garbage piled up in your life. I've addressed that problem in my earlier book, *Risky Living*. Jesus never reacted like that because He didn't have any garbage cluttering up His subconscious. As a result, He was able to hear His critics clearly, and respond to them positively—with love.

Some place I read of a little boy who was punished by his mother. The child reacted in anger, and the mother locked him in her clothes closet until he cooled off. Instead of cooling off, he heated up. Finally the noise in the closet subsided and there was a long period when the mother heard nothing. She opened the door to check on him. He was sitting on the floor.

"What are you doing?" she asked.

He looked up, his eyes still blazing with anger.

"I've spit on your dress. I've spit on your coat. I've spit on your hats. I've spit on your shoes. I'm just sitting here waiting for more spit."

I remember a medical doctor who had suffered a severe

heart attack saying, "I am at the mercy of the man who can make me angry."

And he was. Several months after he made that statement, another doctor criticized him at a hospital staff meeting. He rose to his feet seething with rage, had another heart attack, and dropped to the floor dead.

Anger is one reaction none of us can afford. Spit is too expensive to waste on shoes. Returning love for hate is not only spiritual—it just might save our lives.

Several months ago I visited a saintly old couple who are in the sunset years of life. In fact, the old man is now bedridden, unable to move off his bed without help. Although his mind is still sharp and his spirits good, he needs twenty-four-hour-a-day care for his physical needs.

I had dropped by their house after learning that his only son by a previous marriage—the last of his blood line—had been killed in an accident. I knew the news had come as a great shock and I wanted to reaffirm my love and pray for him. After a few minutes with him beside his bed, I prayed and then walked back into the kitchen where his wife of many years was busy peeling carrots.

"I'll be back," I told her, squeezing her arm.

"That's all right. I know how busy you are," she said sharply. She pulled away from me and grabbed more carrots to peel.

"Why, Dora," I said, surprised. "What's the matter?"

"Nothing!" she lied. "Just get on out of here so I can do my work. Nobody cares about me anyway. Willard gets all the attention. I'm just a slave, a nobody."

"Dora," I said gently, reaching out for her again, "that's not so. I care. A lot of people care."

"Oh, no, they don't," she said, her eyes flashing as she turned to me. "Nobody knows how hard it is on me. All they can think about is Willard back there on that bed. They don't know I have to do his cooking, clean up after him, give him his shots, answer the phone, clean this house. They just walk by me like I didn't even exist."

Once again she pulled away from my grasp and turned on the water in the sink. Her voice was cracking.

"I stood at the door and listened while you prayed for Willard," she said, her back on me to hide her face. "I'm glad you came and know he appreciated it. But your entire prayer was for him. You never even mentioned me—" Her voice broke with anger and she threw her carrots into the sink.

Everything in me wanted to speak out in defense of what I had done. Willard was the one with the grief problem. It was his son who had been killed. This was a time when he needed ministry. Couldn't she understand that? He was back on his bed, his heart broken, and she was in the kitchen feeling sorry for herself because I hadn't mentioned her name in my prayer. What childishness!

I realized, though, that a reaction like that on my part would only drive her deeper into her shell of self-pity. Even though her criticism of what I had done was not justified, I needed to receive it in love. Not only did I need to understand why she felt the way she did, I needed to reach out to try to help her. Additional defensiveness on my part, even if it was given tenderly, would do nothing to help.

I stepped up behind her as she busied herself at the sink, slipping my arms around her waist. "Dora, dear Dora, I love you so much!"

She turned and melted in my arms. Sobbing. Her head against my chest. "Forgive me for being a cranky old woman," she sobbed. "I don't know what we would do without people like you."

The confrontation was over. It had been conquered by love.

The most difficult thing in the world is to look beyond our critic to his need. A black preacher friend of mine says, "Because I can see the potential I can tolerate the apparent." In other words, he has mastered the problem of reacting to his critics because he sees beyond the outer appearance to the inner need—a need he is called to fill even in the lives of his accusers.

It is difficult to move beyond the guilt and condemnation that criticism often dumps on us. How easy it is to remember in vivid detail the face of our critic, to remind ourselves over and over of the exact words he used when he was denouncing us. We remember the set of his mouth and the glint of his eye. We remember the way his knuckles went white while he was talking to us. And we react to the critic far more than we do to his criticism.

"You're saying that because you are like that," we spit back. In the process, we confuse the criticism with the critic. Not only are we unable to see the critic the way he really is, we aren't able to hear the criticism the way we should. Like many differences of opinions on issues, we allow the confrontation to digress from principle to personality, and begin to throw knives at each other, rather than at the issues. If we are to grow, and if we are to help others grow, we must quickly learn to separate the issues from personalities.

"What right does she have to point out things in my life," we cry, "she ought to look at her own life."

"Let him clean up his own mess and then I can hear him," we say with a sneer.

And so we excuse ourselves from ever hearing the message, because we see flaws in the messenger.

Most reaction to hostile criticism comes when we are vulnerable, either at fault or weary from some other battle. Unable to cope adequately, we react in anger. Far better is to react by admitting our inabilities. If I lose my composure, get a twitch in my face, raise my voice in anger, or feel my eyes dilating, then I know I am out of spiritual control. I may have had a good word to share, but if I lose composure then I become ineffective. At such times there is no other way out except to bow my head, let the other person take the lead, and respond with love. Such a procedure not only disarms my critic, but it kills the argument. Again, how can you argue with someone who admits he was wrong?

There is a great deal of tension in the description John gives us of Jesus—a man "full of grace and truth." Grace is at one end of the spectrum, truth at the other. Jesus is the bridge between the two, giving us the ability to cope. The ability to love.

Two years ago I was invited to lead an interdenominational conference for missionaries in Thailand. Sponsored by an ad hoc committee, it was the first time the various Protestant and evangelical missionaries had ever come together with the Roman Catholic priests and nuns for a teaching retreat. Almost one hundred missionaries were involved, coming not only from Thailand, but also from Burma, Malaysia, and other parts of Southeast Asia. We met at the Baptist encampment at Pataya on the Gulf of Siam for the three days of teaching, ministering, and living together. The first day was tense as some of the evangelicals, with their rigid fundamentalism, were forced to interface with the

Roman Catholics. However, by the end of the second day the atmosphere had cleared and it seemed the groups were actually going to be able to flow together in some kind of unity.

The final afternoon, meeting in a large, screened pavilion overlooking the gulf, I spoke on forgiveness. At the close of my teaching session, even before I left the speaker's stand, a Roman Catholic nun stepped forward from the group. She was French, and had been a missionary to the Thai people for a number of years. She knelt before me and crossed herself.

"For many years I had held deep grudges against the Protestants who came into Thailand and built on the foundations laid by the Catholic church. I have been highly critical and I need forgiveness. Will you pray for me?"

I started to respond, for it was the very subject I had been teaching about. But as I stepped forward to pray for her, I felt checked. I stepped back and heard myself saying, "No, sister, I am not the one to pray for you. You have made your confession and now you are absolved from your sin. I want to ask those here who have felt resentment or bitterness toward you to come and pray for you. I want them to come forward, lay hands on you, and bless you. In so doing, they will receive forgiveness themselves."

I stepped to one side and left her kneeling on the concrete floor of the screened pavilion where we were meeting. At once several people got to their feet and came forward. Then several others. In all there were almost a dozen men and women who stood around the kneeling nun, their hands resting gently on her head and shoulders, as they prayed for her—and for themselves. It was a touching moment. There were very few dry eyes in the room.

When the prayer was over, those who had laid hands on the Catholic sister embraced her and started back for their seats. I stepped forward to close the meeting with a prayer when a man on the front row stood up. I recognized him as a medical doctor with the Christian and Missionary Alliance. He spoke out.

"Before we leave, I have something I want to say. I have been in Thailand for eight years. During that time I felt our group were the only spiritual people in the nation. Like Sister Rene, I have been highly critical of others, not only the Catholics but the Pentecostals. I have been wrong. I ask forgiveness of all of you."

His voice was choking as he sat down. Immediately there were three other people on their feet, all trying to speak at once, all confessing their bad attitudes and critical natures and asking forgiveness. They finally slowed down long enough to take turns, but by the time they had finished, others were standing. I stepped back to one side and let the meeting carry itself. We were there for almost another forty-five minutes, as these missionaries, some of whom had been in Thailand for many years, confessed their bad attitudes and made things right with one another.

Finally it seemed we were finished. I stepped back up to the front to once again try to close the meeting. When I did, one other man, on the very back row, stood up. His face was hard, his lips white with anger.

"I have been sitting here for almost an hour," he said, "while all this garbage has been going on. I have tried as hard as I could to keep my mouth shut. But I must speak."

There was not a sound. No one turned around and

looked at him. Every face was forward. Some had their eyes closed as if in prayer. Even the birds outside the pavilion which had accompanied the confession and forgiveness with their songs were suddenly quiet. It was as though the Spirit of God had suddenly been removed from the entire area—leaving a great vacuum. I wondered what would rush in to fill it.

The man continued. "My father was an evangelical missionary in Colombia, South America. I was raised on the mission field. I can remember, as an eight-year-old boy, hiding with my parents behind a clump of bushes while a mob of Roman Catholics, led by the local priest, brought torches and set fire to the little church building my father had built with his own hands."

The man paused, his voice cracking with emotion, holding onto the back of the chair in front of him with fingers white from pressure. He continued.

"The next year I was with my father in the mountains of Colombia. We were visiting an old man who was dying of tuberculosis. Just three weeks before the man had accepted Christ as his Savior and allowed my father to pray with him.

"That afternoon, after we had walked three hours to reach his little hut, we were sitting beside his bed and my father was reading the Bible to him. Suddenly the Roman Catholic priest burst into the hut, followed by three other men who stood just inside the room with their arms folded across their chests. The priest grabbed the old man on the bed and pulled him onto the floor.

" 'If you do not renounce this false religion,' he said sternly, 'you will be excommunicated from the church and denied entrance into heaven when you die.'

"I was too frightened to remain, and I ran from the hut

in tears. My father stayed to argue, but was told he should leave if he valued his life. He had no business interfering with the affairs of the church."

The man stopped speaking and looked around the room. A few heads had turned and were now looking at him. "That is the reason I cannot tolerate what has been taking place here this afternoon," he said. "If you had been hurt by the Roman Catholics as deeply as I have, you would understand."

There was not a sound. He stood, physically shaking, trying to recover his composure enough to sit down. Before he could, however, one of the old Catholic priests on the front row stood to his feet. He turned to the man and began to speak, slowly but deliberately.

"My son, many years ago I was just out of school and went as a missionary to Colombia. It is very possible I was there when you were there—for I am now an old man and you are still young. It matters not, for at that time I had been trained to believe that all evangelicals and Protestants were heretics. I do not know if I was the one who came into that old man's house—but it could have very well been me, for I did many things like that."

He paused, and looked around at the group. Every eye was on him as he spoke. "But many changes have taken place since then. There have been changes in the Roman Catholic church. Thanks to Pope John and others, a new wind of the Holy Spirit is now blowing through the church. No longer are we militant. No longer are we exclusive. Now we see you not as our enemies, but as our brothers. And not only has there been a change in the church, but there has been a change in me. Three years ago, as an old priest, I was baptized in the Holy Spirit and began to speak in tongues. My life is now completely different and I have been praying for the opportunity to confess my sins of those years past and, in some way, to atone for them. Now I ask you, my son, to forgive. Forgive the Roman Catholic church. Forgive me."

He pushed aside his chair and started back toward where the missionary was standing. But before he had gotten through one row of chairs, the man came rushing to meet him, shoving aside chairs to grab him in a tight, tearful embrace. The other people in the group came rushing toward them to form a huge knot in the middle of the room—a mass of loving, forgiving, weeping, laughing believers.

Love had not only prevented a war. It had negotiated the peace.

The man or woman who is secure in the Lord, who knows who he or she is, should have no trouble projecting love toward the critic—be it just criticism or unjust. When Jesus came before Pilate, the Bible says, "He opened not his mouth." He knew who he was.

Pilate railed against him: "They say you are the son of God. Are you the son of God?"

Jesus finally said softly, "That's right. You said it."

That's all He needed to say. He didn't need to outline His doctrine, explain His theology, or quote Scripture. He just stood there.

God is sovereign and intends to fulfill His purpose in creation. Paul wrote to Timothy, "God wishes all men to be saved and come to the knowledge of the truth." That means God has a purpose for every man—for every situation.

Israel was not chosen just to be God's favorite people. They were chosen for a purpose. That purpose was to be a light to the Gentiles.

Jesus came not only to die, to rise from the grave, and to save us from our sins so we can go to heaven. He came to send His Spirit into the church and the church into the world. That was His purpose.

The message of the New Testament is not a summons to human effort. Rather, it is a declaration of God's intention. The New Testament is not a book of baseball ground rules nor is it simply "The Manufacturer's Handbook." The New Testament is an eternal declaration of the purpose of God.

The Bible does not speak of a plan. In fact, the word "plan" does not even appear in the King James Version. But the Bible has a great deal to say about God's "purpose." He is moving with deliberate speed to fulfill that purpose in our lives.

Trials and joys, suffering and glory, critics and criticism are all part of that purpose. The day will come when Jesus will return and the love of God will cover the earth as the waters cover the sea. When that happens, there will be no more need for critics—or their criticism—for we shall be as He is. Until then, all creation is groaning, or as Phillips translates Romans 8:19, "standing on tip-toe" awaiting the manifestation of the sons of God.

In the meantime, the Holy Spirit is busy conforming us to the image of God's Son. Critics—and their criticism—are His finest tools.